Bristol Radical Pa

Walter Virgo and the Blakeney Gang

The struggle against enclosure in the Forest of Dean in the latter part of the nineteenth century

Ian Wright

ISBN 978-1-911522-26-3

Bristol Radical History Group. 2nd Edition 2017.
1st Edition 2013.
www.brh.org.uk ~ brh@brh.org.uk

And ye who find pasture for sheep and for ass,
For pig and for pony, on good Forest grass,
Yield not your possessions, hold fast to your right,
Or soon it will vanish, with more, from your sight,
For easy enough it is to foretell
They'll suck out the egg if they once-prick the shell!

(Anon.) The Foresters' Egg! A Timely Warning!
Dean Forest Mercury, 23 May 1884.

Sheep around a pit shaft on Fair Play in the Forest of Dean.

Contents

Maps iv
Introduction 1
The Seeds of Revolt 4
Historical Background 4
1831 Dean Riot 6
Poaching 7
The Judicial System 11
Areas Targeted by Poachers 14
Aftermath of the 1831 Riot 16
The Forest under Campbell (1854-1893) 17
Working Conditions 19
Unity between Commoners and Miners 21
Industrial Unrest 24
Rebellion 26
The Forest under Baylis (1893 -1906) 26
Walter Virgo 27
Petty Crime 28
Guerrilla Warfare 29
Riot in Lydney 32
The Davis Family 33
Accusations against Virgo 35
Rebellion in Blakeney 36
Petition against the Gang 38
Death of a Policeman 39
Fowls, ducks and geese. 42
Dynamite 44
United Deep Colliery Gale 44
Arson Attack 46
The Long Affray 47
Moses Virgo 49
The Commoners Get Organised 49
Conclusion 52
An Organised Working Class 54
Modern Times 56
Appendix: Blakeney Gang Court Records 1870 -1899 60
Sources 67
Books and Journal Articles 67
Newspapers 69
Picture Credits 70
Acknowledgements 70

Maps

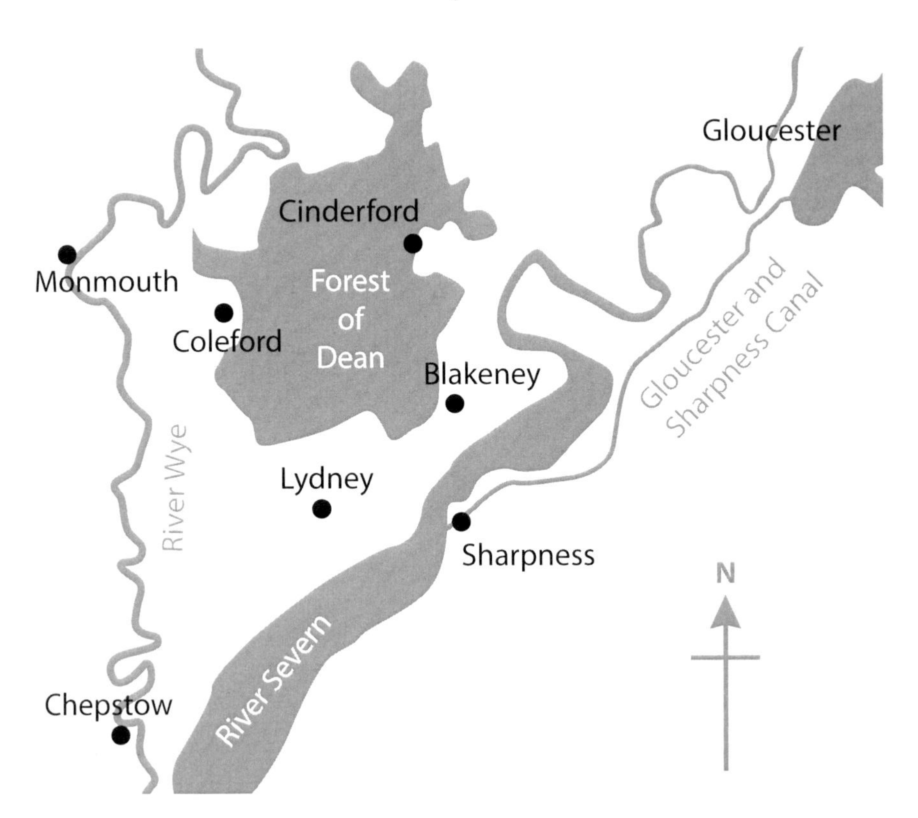

The Forest of Dean and Gloucester.
The central shaded area is the Statutory Forest of Dean

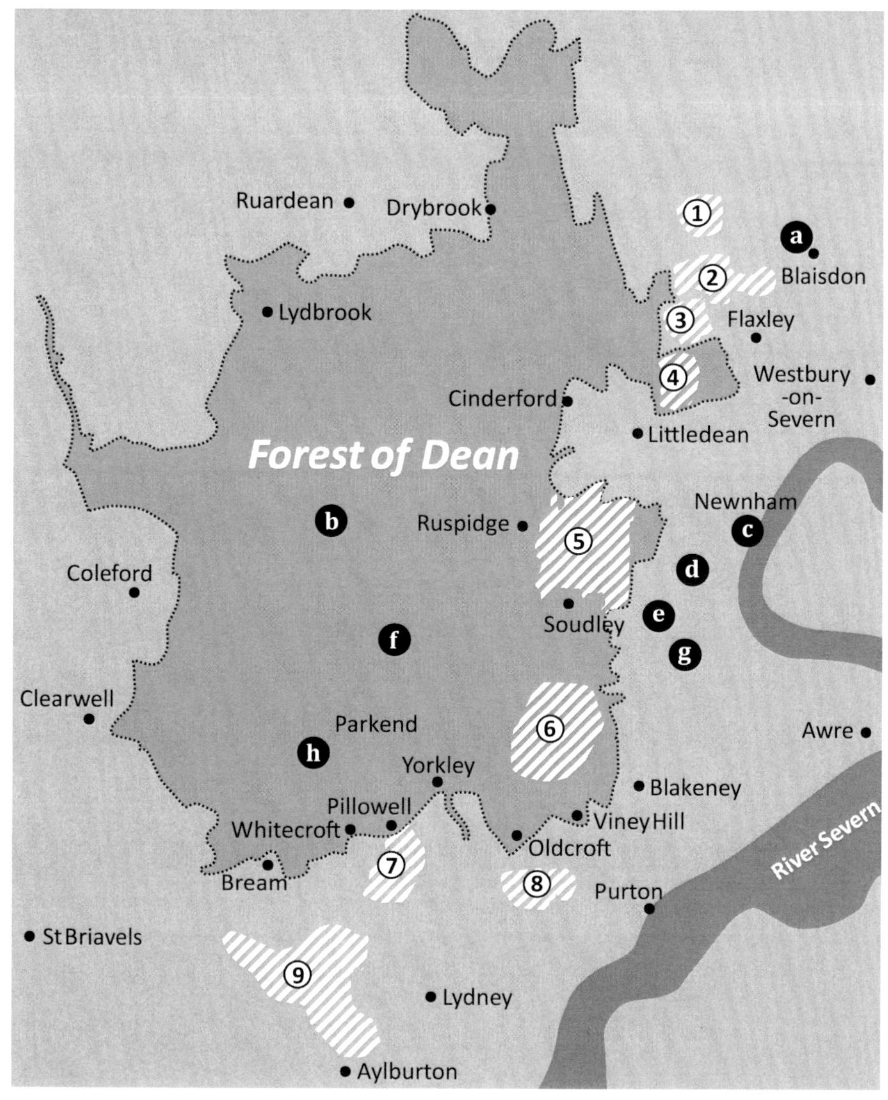

The Forest of Dean and surrounding area.

Places
a. Blaisdon Hall
b. The Speech House
c. Riverdale
d. Arams Farm
e. The Haie
f. New Fancy Pit in Russell's Enclosure
g. Oaklands
h. Whitemead Park

Woods
1. Hope Wood
2. Flaxley Woods
3. Welshbury Wood
4. Chestnuts Hill
5. Abbotswood
6. Blakeney Hill
7. Kidnalls Wood
8. Horage Wood & Purlieu Wood
9. Lydney Park Estate

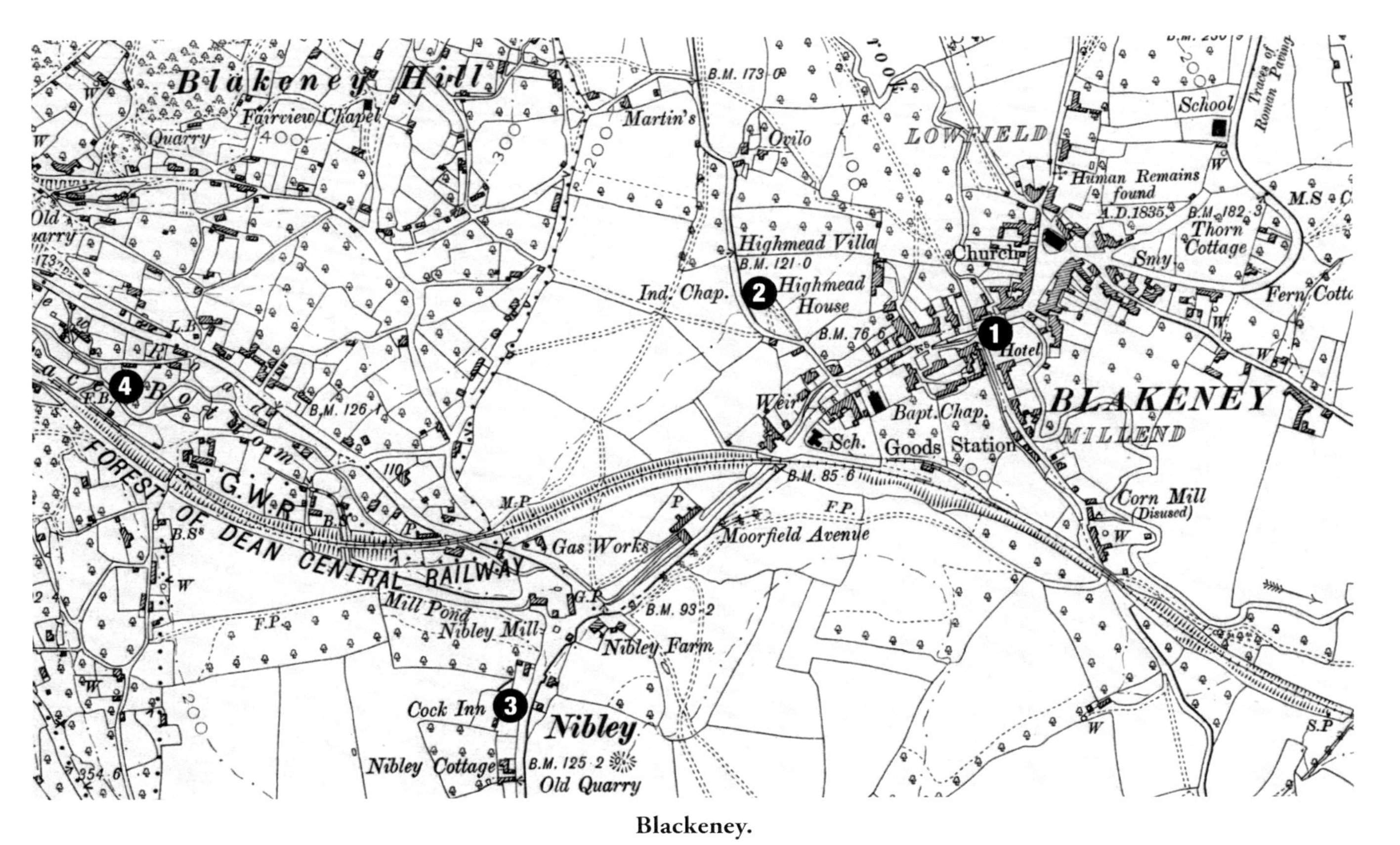

Blackeney.

1 The Kings Head Public House. 2 The Tabernacle Chapel. 3 The Cock Inn. 4 Furnace Bottom site of the death of PC Morris

Introduction

In the early 1890s, local and national newspapers reported that a gang of 'ruffians' were exerting a reign of terror over the local inhabitants in the Blakeney area of the Forest of Dean. Letters appeared in the papers warning that a situation of extreme lawlessness had arisen and claiming that the disorder was far worse than in Ireland.[1] Incidents involving poisoning, maiming, stealing, poaching, midnight raids, dynamiting, arson and murder were reported in the press. One family in particular, headed by Walter Virgo, who by custom ran his flock of sheep on the local Crown land, was accused by government officials of being behind the disorder.[2]

The events became known as the Blakeney Outrages. At the time, the authorities quickly characterised the men involved as belonging to a gang of criminal thugs, emphasising their use of intimidation and violence. It was clear that their actions were both desperate and dangerous and at times violent. Nevertheless, this pamphlet will argue that the Blakeney Outrages of the 1890s can best be understood as part of the on-going struggle in defence of the commons and against enclosure in the Forest of Dean, which had in the past resulted in violent confrontations between Foresters and the authorities. In this context the commons refers to the natural resources which have historically been held collectively and not owned privately such as common land, minerals, rivers and game. Enclosure refers to appropriation of the commons by the state or private individuals.

Historically there have been a number of attempts to completely enclose the Forest of Dean and put its resources out of reach of those who live and work there. The first significant attempt occurred in the seventeenth century and the next in the early nineteenth century. More recently we have seen attempts in 2011 and 2014 to privatise the Forest, which were successfully resisted by Hands off Our Forest.[3] All of these challenges met with strong collective

1 At this time the Irish countryside was in revolt as a direct consequence of the recent catastrophic famine and excessive rents and evictions by absentee landlords. Agrarian outrages and terrorist acts had spread to many counties, provoking violent confrontations between landowners and their henchmen and desperate tenant farmers and resulting in deaths on both sides. See Clark, S. *Social Origins of the Irish Land War*, Guildford: Princeton Legacy Library, 2014.

2 The Crown owned most of the Statutory Forest of Dean which also includes some private land. Forest is a territory, usually unenclosed, and not necessarily woodland but often covered with woods of varying density, but also included heathland, wood pasture, arable and even villages. It was designated by perambulation and used by the sovereign for his or her hunting and subject to forest law. In early centuries, forest virtually meant the King's hunting ground when the protection of deer and their habitat was paramount.

3 http://www.handsoffourforest.org/

resistance with varying degrees of success. However this pamphlet will discuss the struggle in the latter part of the nineteenth century which resulted in covert actions and violent confrontations between the Crown and commoners in the Blakeney area. In particular, the pamphlet will discuss how the customary right to common, that is the right of an individual to graze animals in the Forest, came under attack. In addition, the pamphlet will consider how the customary right to hunt for game became criminalised.[4]

Chris Fisher, in his book Fisher C. *Custom, Work and Market Capitalism, The Forest of Dean Colliers, 1788-1888*, places the disturbances firmly within the conflict over customary rights within the Forest of Dean. He discovered the story in the records and letters of the Deputy Surveyor, the Commissioner of Woods and the local clergy as well as a range of local newspapers.[5] None of these sources would be expected to be sympathetic to the plight of poor commoners who were directly confronting the authorities. Therefore it is no surprise that their actions were characterised as pure criminality and the people involved as a 'bad lot'.

Simon Sandall has explored the idea of collective memory and its relation to the organisation of popular protest in defence of the commons and against enclosure in the Forest of Dean from the seventeenth century onwards.[6] Sandall describes how this tradition has been passed down the generations and became an accepted part of the common culture in the Forest. This pamphlet will consider how the actions of some Foresters became more desperate and violent in the second half of the nineteenth century in response to increasing industrialisation and changing social relations. Many Foresters believed that they had the right to run their animals on Crown land and hunt game in the local woods. They fought hard to defend these rights at a time when their activities and protests were increasingly criminalised. As a result, crime became tied up with the social conflicts and the antagonisms associated with these changes.

4 The seminal works on 'customary rights' are Thompson, E. P. *Whigs and Hunters: The Origin of the Black Act,* London: Breviary Stuff Publications, 2013. Thompson, E. P. *Customs in Common: Studies in Traditional Popular Culture,* New Press. 1993. Hay, D., Linebaugh, P., Rule, J.G., Thompson, E.P. and C Winslow, C. *Albion's Fatal Tree: Crime and Society in Eighteenth-Century England,* London: Verso Press, 2012 and Bushaway, B. *By Rite: Custom, Ceremony and Community in England 1700-1880,* London: Breviary Stuff Publications, 2010.
5 The Commissioners of Woods, Forests and Land Revenues were the officials under the United Kingdom Crown, charged with the management of Crown lands.
6 Sandall, S. *Custom and Popular Memory in the Forest of Dean 1550 – 1832*, Scholar Press, 2013.
Collective memory refers to the collection of memories shared by a common culture and passed down generations.

The pamphlet will also argue that in general, but with some exceptions, the Blakeney Outrages can be understood fruitfully as social crimes. Crime is sometimes regarded as social when it represents a conscious challenge to a prevailing social order and its values. Historians describe such actions as social crime. This includes forms of popular action and custom such as poaching, wood theft, food riots and smuggling, which were criminalized by the ruling class, but were not regarded as blameworthy, either by those committing them, or by the communities from which they came.[7] In spite of the title, the pamphlet will argue that to characterize the commoners of Blakeney who took part in these events as a 'gang' is to simply criminalise their actions without placing them in any social or historical context. It will contend that the existence of a specific single criminal gang was unlikely. The pamphlet will argue that the events were a result of a response to changing social and economic conditions and access to the commons. In this way we may begin to understand the political nature of the Blakeney disturbances, the contested nature of crime, and how the disorder was located within the structural contexts of the changing nature of society.[8]

The same men who were developing trade union organisation in the mines and quarries could be out poaching at night or running sheep on the Crown enclosures. In doing so they often ran into direct conflict with the authorities at work and at home at a time when their customary rights were being curtailed and they were having to accept their new status as employees working for outside capitalists.[9] The pamphlet will reflect upon how the inequality, poverty and exploitation of the labouring poor were central to the development of an organised working class in the Forest of Dean with roots in this historical struggle over customary rights.

The first section of this pamphlet will examine the underlying social, political and historical currents leading up to the disturbances in Blakeney. The second section will consider how these tensions erupted into outright rebellion during the 1890s in the Blakeney area.

7 Hobsbawn, E. J. *Primitive Rebels: Studies in Archaic Forms of Social Movement in the 19th and 20th Centuries*, WW Norton, 1959. Please note social crime is not 'good crime' and sometimes can involve acts of violence.

8 See the European Group for the Study of Deviance & Social Control at http://www.europeangroup.org/?q=node/7

9 Cannock Chase is another area of the country where mining and poaching went hand in hand. See Hay, D. *Albion's Fatal Tree, Poaching and the Game Laws on Cannock Chase* in Hay, D. et al. (2012). See also Peter Linebaugh who outlines these changes in the urban setting in Linebaugh, P. *The London Hanged: Crime and Civil Society in the Eighteenth Century*, London: Verso Press. 2006.

The Seeds of Revolt

Historical Background

The right to common, pannage and estovers had been claimed by the people of the Forest of Dean for centuries.[10] Pannage refers to the right to feed pigs in the Forest following the fall of acorns and beech-masts. Estover refers to the right to collect firewood and small timbers. Free mining rights had been granted by the Crown at least as far back as 1244. These allowed any son of a free miner working for a year and a day in a Forest pit and born within the Hundred of St Briavels to open a mine anywhere in the Forest. These were usually small drift mines which were distinct from the large deep pits developed in the nineteenth century and financed by outside capitalists. Similar rights existed for quarrying.

In the Middle Ages, the Forest was used as a royal hunting ground and local laws dealt with the regulation of the Forest vert and venison for the protection of timber and the deer.[11] However, despite its gradual appropriation by the Crown, the Foresters treated the Forest as their own, drawing sustenance from its woods and wasteland above the surface and from minerals below, in particular coal and iron ore. Timber was used in coal mines and for building. Coppiced wood was used to make charcoal for iron smelting and for fuel.

In past centuries, any attempt to enclose the Forest had been sufficient to cause serious disturbances and fences and mounds would be quickly destroyed. The seventeenth century witnessed a two-pronged assault on Forest custom from both changing Crown policies and the opportunism of private individuals, some of whom were members of the local gentry. In particular the leasing of ironworks from the Crown required a supply of cordwood for charcoal and led to increased plundering of forest resources. The leasing not only impeded the exercise of mining custom, but also disrupted common rights to grazing and fuel. Major riots took place during this period resulting in fences being destroyed and the right to common asserted. The preface of *In Contempt of All Authority*, Buchanan Sharp's book which deals with the seventeenth century Dean Forest Riots, concludes:

> That in times of economic and social distress or political dislocation (such as the Civil War) the "lower orders" of Tudor and Stuart England were provoked into self-organised direct action by very basic issues of food supply, employment and common rights. In

10 Linebaugh, P. *The Magna Carta Manifesto*, London: University of California Press, 2008.

11 Vert refers to all vegetation in a forest protected by forest law.

> the course of such actions they manifested an intense hatred of the gentry and well-to-do, whom they held responsible for their existing conditions.[12]

In the second part of the seventeenth century the Crown sought to prioritise the Forest as a source of timber for the construction of ships for the navy. In 1668, an Act was passed which authorised the enclosure of areas of the Forest up to a maximum of 11,000 acres for timber production. At this time the Statutory Forest of Dean covered approximately 21,000 acres. As long as areas of woodland were enclosed, the Crown claimed that these areas were exempted from all rights including those of common, mining and quarrying. However, when the young trees in an enclosure were big enough to be safe from grazing animals, the enclosure could be thrown open and an equivalent area enclosed elsewhere. In addition, Foresters could run their animals and mine and quarry within the remaining 10,000 acres of Crown land which included forest waste, unenclosed woodland and roadside verges.[13] In spite of this, the conflict continued throughout the eighteenth century.

In 1723, the government passed the Black Act which was enacted purportedly against people known in Berkshire and Hampshire as the Blacks, who were hunting deer at night and in disguise. Once the Act was law, it was used against a wide range of crimes against property, eventually leading to approximately 50 capital offences including being armed within a forest, chase or royal park while disguised or with a blacked face. It became an offence to hunt, kill, wound or steal deer in these locations, with the first offence punishable by a fine, and the second by penal transportation. An offender could be executed if he set fire to corn, hay, straw, wood, houses or barns, killed cattle or shot another person. Other offences included fishing, the hunting of hares, the destruction of fish-ponds, the destruction of trees, etc. As a result, the authorities began to characterise resistance to enclosure in terms of criminality and started to use the term 'gang' to describe those involved in the disorder. In 1735, violence erupted over the impounding of commoners' animals by the Crown and access to resources in the Forest of Dean.

> Whereas a notorious and villainous gang of persons have several times of late assembled themselves together in a riotous manner

12 Sharp, B. *In Contempt of All Authority – Rural Artisans and Riot in the West of England, 1586 -1660*, London: Breviary Stuff Publications, 2010.

13 Forest waste is the name given to non-forested areas of Crown land in the Forest of Dean. It has traditionally been grazed by commoners' animals which has maintained its open character and unique ecology.

> and committed diverse disorders by breaking open the pounds at the Castle of St Briavels and Park End Lodge, and discharged from thence several cattle. And upon Saturday night, the 5th instant, the same gang came to the Lodge of Mr R. Worgan, entered his garden, beat down his beans, cut up his cabbages and apple trees, broke his windows, and part of the pound wall; then adjourned to the Speech House Lodge which is in the possession of George James, commonly called Captain Whithorne. Upon their coming they immediately fell to work on the Pound, but being desired by the Captain to desist who rose to the window to disperse themselves, they returned him for answer a brace of slugs in at the window. The Captain upon that ply'd them warmly with small shot, who sent him in return a great quantity of slugs and balls, so that almost a continual fire lasted for nearly half an hour, when their ammunition being spent, they had something else to pick besides stones out of the pound wall. On the morrow one of the gang was taken and on Monday committed by Thomas Pyrke Esq. to Gloucester Castle; but his company being apprised of it, seven of them disguised themselves in a dreadful manner, and armed with four guns and three swords, came several miles over the Forest but finding their comrade gone too long before, returned back to pull off their two ragged petticoats and clean off their too much like Devil's faces. But it is to be hoped the gentlemen of the county will lend an assisting hand to put a stop to these desperate and resolute fellows. N.B. They are supposed to be what are called Fanside men, and come from in or about Clowerwell.[14]

The Black Act was finally repealed in 1823 but conflict associated with poaching, wood stealing, mining and enclosure continued. The passing of the Night Poaching Act of 1828 meant that men caught at night and armed with offensive weapons with the intention of destroying game were still liable to transportation.

1831 Dean Riot

In 1831, riots, led by Warren James, broke out again and enclosure fences across the Forest were torn down. The Foresters fought to resist the twin onslaught from the Crown, which sought to enclose the Forest so as to produce more timber for the navy, and from businessmen who sought industrial profits from minerals in the ground. This was a culmination of troubles that had been escalating for

14 *Gloucester Journal* 22 July 1735. Clowerwell (now Clearwell) is a small village in the Forest of Dean.

a quarter of a century. The Crown and outside capitalists wanted to introduce the free market and the right of property on land in the Forest and its mineral resources. To achieve this, they sought to curtail the free miners' rights and the right to common. The Crown had enclosed up to the maximum of 11,000 acres but failed to throw open the enclosures when the trees had matured.[15] These enclosures effectively forced local men off their land and free mines to work as wage labourers for the new capitalist mine owners. Some were reduced to unemployment and poverty. The revolt was ultimately suppressed by military force. Warren James was sentenced to death, but this was later commuted to transportation for life.[16]

In 1841, Warren James died an early death in poverty and destitution in Tasmania. In contrast, the Crown agent in the Forest at the time of the riots, Deputy Surveyor Edward Machen, retired in 1854. A huge retirement celebration and grand dinner were held at Speech House to which all the Forest dignitaries were invited. Richard Daniels, chairman of Hands Off Our Forest and the Forest of Dean Free Miners Association recently said:

> Inadvertently this provided a Forest hero in the form of Warren James, free miner, who led the riots and paid a high price for his leadership. Warren is still remembered today for his determination to protect commoning and the tradition.[17]

Poaching

The tradition of hunting for game in the Forest of Dean goes back to time immemorial. For the majority of the poor, hunting was seen as a customary right which provided them with food. In medieval times hunting on Crown land was subject to the game laws to protect the deer for the King's hunt. However in 1217 the Charter of the Forests conceded that no man was to lose life or limb for poaching the King's deer. As a result, poaching was common with apprehended offenders usually being sent to prison for not more than a few

15 Oliver Rackham is scathing about the destruction of the rich and complex ancient woodland and wood pasture by the nineteenth century Dean enclosures. Most of the ancient coppices and pollards were completely destroyed. Rackham, O. *The History of the Countryside*, London: Phoenix Press, 1986, p.147.

16 See Anstis, R. *Warren James and Dean Forest Riots*, London: Breviary Stuff Publications, 2012 and Wright I. *The Life and Times of Warren James: Free Miner of The Forest Of Dean* Bristol: BRHG, 2008.

17 Fisher C. *Custom, Work and Market Capitalism. The Forest of Dean Colliers, 1788-1888*. London: Breviary Stuff Publications, 2016, p ix. The Speech House was built in 1676 by the King as a "court" where local people could have their say. The people of the Forest of Dean have continued to meet there to discuss issues of collective concern.

The Poachers by Henry Alken Walsh.

months. Even the local barons and knights were involved.[18]

This changed when the Crown and surrounding landowners sought to enclose the land to claim it as private property and sought profits from timber production, agriculture or the leasing of hunting licenses to the wealthy. Customary hunting of game became trespass and theft.[19] In the eighteenth century, the Black Act was used against deer poachers in the Forest. As a result, the exercise of customary right started to turn ugly and resulted in rioting.[20]

In addition, the theft of cattle, horses and sheep from private individuals had become a problem and was treated very seriously by the authorities. This led to six hangings in Gloucester in the year 1800 alone.[21] As the century progressed the sentences became less severe. In August 1833 Stephen Edwards (age 21) and Richard Drew (age 24) from Clearwell were transported for life for stealing a lamb.[22] In March 1850, Frederick Powell of Blakeney Hill was transported for 10 years for stealing a ewe.[23]

18 Birrell, J. "Aristocratic Poachers in the Forest of Dean: their methods, their quarry and their companions", *Transactions of the Bristol and Gloucestershire Archaeological Society*, Vol. 119 (2001), p. 147-154.
19 Also see Mills, S. *Poaching in the South West, The Berkeley Case*, Bristol: BRHG, 2015.
20 Thompson, E. P. *Whigs and Hunters: The Origin of the Black Act,* London: Breviary Stuff Publications, 2013, p. 246.
21 http://www.capitalpunishmentuk.org
22 *Gloucestershire Chronicle* 17 August 1833.
23 *Monmouthshire Beacon* 30 March 1850.

In the early nineteenth century, poaching of deer on Crown land was widespread and poachers often fought bloody battles with gamekeepers and watchers and risked imprisonment, transportation or even death for their activities. In the years 1839–1848, the local Petty Sessions dealt with 95 cases of offences against the deer and 17 charges concerning assaults upon the keepers.[24] In 1849, Deputy Surveyor, Sir James Campbell reported:[25]

> Since I have been at Dean Forest, keepers and others have been absolutely killed by poachers. One man certainly was killed since I was there; that was a policeman. They took to shooting the keepers when they were not allowed to shoot the deer and it was thought better to give the deer up.[26]

Some coal mine owners were also concerned about the level of poaching and saw the deer as a threat to the discipline of their workforce. They needed a flexible labour force ready to submit to the discipline of working for hire and this could only become possible if independent means of survival were closed down. In 1849, the coal pit owner Thomas Nicholson argued:

> I think the effect of the deer is very bad upon the general habits and morals of the population: if once a man begins to poach, we can never reckon upon them working afterwards.[27]

In 1855, the Crown solved the problem in the Forest of Dean by having all the deer killed under the 1851 Deer Removal Act. The Crown was now happy to have all animals cleared from the enclosures as it was mainly interested in timber production. However, after the removal of deer, poachers continued to hunt rabbits, hares and pheasants in the Crown woods and in the estates of the local landowners surrounding the Forest. Sheep belonging to local farmers also became a target. In August 1861, four men out poaching and who were suspected of attempting to steal sheep, were confronted by Police Sergeant Beard in a field near Speech House. In the confrontation that followed Beard was attacked and later died. The men were soon arrested and sentenced to 15 years penal servitude.[28] Nationally and in areas surrounding the Forest the conflict

24 Report from the Select Committee on the Woods, Forests and Land Revenues of the Crown 1849, XX (SCW) appendix 42. cited in Fisher C. (2016), p. 44.

25 Deputy Surveyor is the government official whose responsibility is the administration of the Forest.

26 SCW p. 31, cited in Fisher, C. (2016), p. 44.

27 cited by Fisher, C. *The Independent Collier,* Sussex: Harvester Press, 1978, p. 39.

28 http://www.gloucestershirepolicemuseum.co.uk/page_2346438.html.

continued throughout the nineteenth century and in the 1890s there were still reports of deaths on both sides. Harry Hopkins refers to "this long affray" as being more like a guerrilla war.[29] For the labouring poor in the 1890s, poaching on private land could still be a matter of survival and it was no surprise that many local men came into conflict with landowners, their gamekeepers and the police. Historian, David Jones, wrote that the poacher was:

> such an ordinary figure, an accepted and normal part of rural life. In the second quarter of the nineteenth century poaching was widely regarded as one of the fastest growing crimes in Britain, and, unlike arson, highway robbery, cattle, horse, and sheep-stealing, it continued to be a prominent and permanent part of the rural scene even in the 1880s and 1890s.[30]

Poachers were overwhelmingly working people and in the Forest of Dean usually colliers. Poaching was a classic case of a social crime which the magistrates and the landowners were determined to stamp out. However ordinary Foresters for the most part would not think poaching was a crime at all. Douglas Hay's study showed how local communities:

> ...united solidly in defence of poaching. The keepers met with a wall of silence when they tried to make inquiries, but found that word spread like lightning when they obtained a search warrant, and that the suspects had escaped with 'the apparatus' just before they arrived. Witnesses lost their memories... Poachers not only gave alibis for one another; they also took measures against informers.[31]

Quite often village communities would rally around and support members accused of poaching. At the same time there was hostility towards local gamekeepers who were seen to be protecting the interests of the landed gentry. William Stinchcombe worked as a gamekeeper for Wyndham Quin on his Clearwell Estate in the Forest of Dean in the 1870s. In November 1876, an armed man was discovered by Stinchcombe poaching pheasants on Quin's game reserve at Bearse Common. Stinchcombe followed the poacher but when he was within twenty yards the man turned around and shot him in the legs.

29 Hopkins, H. *The Long Affray, The Poaching Wars in Britain*, London: Faber and Faber, 1985, p. 276-277.
30 Jones, D. Crime, Protest, Community and Police in Nineteenth Century Britain, London: Routledge. 1982.
31 Hay, D. (2012), p. 198.

The severely wounded Stinchcombe made his way to Longley farm where he received medical treatment and survived.[32]

Later in the day Stinchcombe identified the man to Superintendent Chipp as George Morse and claimed that a year before Morse had threatened to put a bar through his head. Morse worked as a miner but was unemployed at the time as a result of a recession in the coal trade. Chipp proceeded to Morse's house in St Briavels where he discovered wet clothes and boots covered in remnants of leaves, gorse and grass. Chipp hid outside the house and a few hours later he noticed a large bundle of food had been thrown over the hedge. Chipp assumed the food was meant for Morse's wife and children who were close to starvation. The next day Chipp examined the site of the crime and discovered that Morse's boots matched the tracks in the ground which also led to Morse's house. The police watched the house night and day but it appeared that Morse had absconded. Morse was eventually arrested in Usk several weeks later. At his trial before Gloucester Assizes in March 1877 a series of witnesses from St Briavels gave statements providing alibis and testaments to Morse's good character. The jury found him not guilty and he was released.[33]

This was not the first time that the use of guns by poachers led to deaths or serious injury. For instance a fatal accident happened in August 1865 when the two Penn brothers from Ruardean were out night poaching in Bircham Grove Enclosure. They were both carrying double barrelled shot guns and it appeared that one boy accidently shot and killed his brother.[34] In another incident in February 1881 Henry Bayton, Thomas Bendle and Thomas Bayton were night poaching with guns in woodland belonging to the Crown at Highmeadow near Staunton. In this case the shooting rights had been let out to Mark Dixon, a local magistrate living at Oak House in Newland. The poachers were confronted by Dixon's head gamekeeper, Webb, and four of his assistants. In the resulting struggle Webb was shot and wounded. As a result Henry Bayton was sentenced to six months hard labour.[35]

The Judicial System

During this period the lowest level of criminal court was the Petty Sessions also known as the County Magistrates Court. The Forest of Dean was split into administrative areas, each with a Petty Sessions which dealt with minor criminal offences. For the more serious offences initial committal proceedings were held in the Magistrates Court. If there was a case to answer, arrested suspects were

32 *Western Daily Press* 20 November 1986.
33 *Gloucester Journal* 31 March 1877.
34 *Gloucester Journal* 18 August 1865.
35 *Gloucester Citizen* 16 February 1881.

then sent to the Quarter Sessions or Assizes for trial. Up to the early nineteenth century, the system of policing was by unpaid parish constables. However in 1839, the County Police Act permitted Justices in County Quarter Sessions to establish police forces in their counties and to appoint paid police officers. According to Geoff Sindrey and Ted Heath:

> The early days of policing in the Forest took place against the background of tension between the free miners, commoners and organised labour on the one hand and capitalist mine-owners and The Crown (Forestry) Commission on the other.[36]

In 1871, Edward Chipp was appointed to the post of Superintendent of the Forest police. In his diary he described the Forest at the time as being more like a "lawless state" and claimed he was sometimes in fear of his life.[37] By the end of the century the number of police stations in the Forest had increased to twenty two. Chipp was based at Coleford, there was an Inspector at Lydney and Sergeants in charge at Blakeney, Cinderford, Littledean and Newnham. At the same time a whole raft of legislation had been introduced which inevitably brought the police into conflict with some members of the local community. For instance, hanging washing in the street, beating a carpet and flying a kite were offences set out in the Town Police Clauses Act (1847) and punishable by a fine. The Licensing Act (1872) could impose a fine and possibly jail for up to 51 weeks for being drunk in charge of a horse or a cow.

Another source of conflict resulted from the claim made by Foresters that they had the right to allow their animals to graze road side verges. Consequently, in the latter part of the century, as industrialisation and the road networks developed, more and more small holders were being brought before the magistrates and fined for allowing their animals to roam or obstruct the highway. As the century progressed activities such as the taking of estovers also became criminalised. For instance in May 1871, Harriet Haywood, Hannah Woodward and Elisa Watkins from Pillowell were charged with taking firewood from Kidnalls Wood, the property of local magistrate, Isaiah Totter, and were sent to prison for one month. In the same month, John Bendell of Pillowell was charged with assaulting John Hunt, a toll keeper from Bream, who caught him with some wood in his arms. Bendell was imprisoned for one month.[38] In these cases conflict over the customary right to collect estovers from the

36 Sindrey, G. and Heath, T. *A Forest Beat, The Forest of Dean Police Force, 1839–2000*, Lydney: Black Dwarf Publications, 2000, p. 17.

37 Ibid p.18.

38 *Gloucester Journal* 13 May 1871.

Forest directly led to violence and prison. Nearly twenty years later William Elsmore, an old man from Whitecroft , was fined 10 shillings or seven days in prison for stealing a small quantity of wood, valued at 3 pennies, from Crown woodland.[39] These types of events were reported on numerous occasions in the local papers during this period with many Foresters being sent to prison for minor offences against property.

Night poaching was considered a far more serious offence by the authorities and earlier in the nineteenth century many offenders were transported. The Poaching Prevention Act (1862) reduced the severity of the sentences and as a result transportation was no longer used as a punishment. Instead, the usual sentence was now a fine of up to £10 or up to four months in prison, with confiscation of poaching equipment. Nevertheless, the fine was equivalent to about two month's wages and could have serious consequences for a family's welfare. Day poaching was considered less serious and usually resulted in a relatively small fine. However, the Act embroiled the police in the poaching conflict by giving them unprecedented powers of stop and search of highway carts and persons suspected of poaching. As a result, the local gentry could now call on the police to assist their gamekeepers to track down and arrest poachers, resulting in more cases being brought to court.

There's blood on your foreign shrubs, squire,
There's blood on your pointer's feet;
There's blood on the game you sell, squire,
And there's blood on the game you eat!
Charles Kingsley, A Rough Rhyme on a Rough Matter, 1848

There were now approximately 22,000 acres, consisting mainly of woodland and forest waste, owned by the Crown making up the Statutory Forest of Dean. In addition there were also large areas of land owned by the landed gentry on estates bordering Crown property. Their woodlands provided ample opportunities for local people to trespass in search of game. However these landowners, including the Crown, were now making a good income from renting out shooting rights to wealthy individuals. As a result, landowners and those renting shooting rights employed a large number of gamekeepers, who had the right to apprehend and identify poachers, to protect their interests. In the last third of the nineteenth century the number of gamekeepers grew by 60 per cent.[40] By 1911, in rural districts, it was calculated that there were twice

39 *Gloucester Journal* 21 March 1896.
40 Hopkins, H (1985) p. 307.

as many gamekeepers as policemen.[41] In addition, the woodmen employed by the Crown were required to keep a lookout for poachers operating within the Statutory Forest. The increase in the number of gamekeepers combined with the involvement of the police in the conflict meant that the number of poachers apprehended increased towards the second half of the nineteenth century that. By 1875, game convictions nationally reached over 10,000 a year, twice the number than thirty years before.[42] Court records for the petty sessions in the Forest reveal an increase in cases of poachers being brought before the magistrates during the period 1880 to 1900 compared to the previous years. However it is reasonable to assume, given the large area of woodland, that this represented only a small proportion of the number of men out poaching.

Areas Targeted by Poachers

Common areas targeted by poachers in the latter part of the nineteenth century around the Blakeney area included the following:

Lydney Park Estate owned by Charles Bathurst (1836-1907) who was a Barrister-at-Law. Shooting rights on the Estate were let out to various wealthy individuals. Bathurst was a County Magistrate for the Lydney Petty Sessional Division.

Welshbury Wood, Hope Wood and Flaxley Wood Copse owned by Sir Thomas Hyde Crawley-Boevey, 5th Baronet (1837-1912). He was High Sheriff of Gloucestershire in 1882. Crawley-Boevey was a County Magistrate for the Newnham Petty Sessional Division which also sat at Littledean.

Abbotswood Estate in Ruspidge owned by the Crawshays who held extensive interests in coal mining and iron works throughout the Forest. Henry Crawshay (1812-1879) lived at Oaklands, Awre. His sons Edwin Crawshay (1836-1902) and William Crawshay (1845-1910) lived at Blaisdon Hall, Blaisdon and Riverdale, Newnham respectively. All three were County Magistrates for the Newnham Petty Sessional Division. In 1899, the Crown purchased the Abbotswood Estate and it then became part of the Statutory Forest.

The Estate of Russell James Kerr (1832- 1910) who was lord of the manors of Newnham and Ruddle. He lived at the Haie near Newnham. In 1910 his son, also Sir Russell James Kerr, (1863-1952) succeeded his father as lord of the manor. Both father and son were County Magistrates for the Newnham Petty Sessional Division.

Sedbury Park Estate which was bought by Sir Samuel Stephens Marling, 1st Baronet (1810-1883) in 1875. Marling was a British cloth manufacturer and Liberal Party politician. At the time the estate covered 5,887 acres and included

41 Hopkins, H (1985) p. 264.
42 Hopkins, H (1985) p. 253.

25 farms in Tidenham, Woolaston, and Hewelsfield and included most of the land between Sedbury and Hewelsfield. Marling was MP for the Forest of Dean (West Gloucestershire) area from 1868–1874. In 1883, the estate was inherited by his son Sir William Henry Marling (1835-1919) who was a County Magistrate for the Lydney Petty Sessional Division.

The Clearwell Estate, which in the nineteenth century was comprised of Clearwell Court and 14 farms and woods between Newland, St. Briavels and Bream covering an area of 2,300 acres. In 1876, the estate was inherited by Windham Henry Wyndham-Quin, who with the trustees conveyed it in 1882 to John Eveleigh Wyndham. In 1893, the Wyndham trustees sold the estate to Henry Collins, whose mortgagees later secured possession.

The river Severn and the river Wye provided ample opportunities for the poaching of fish. This activity was common along most of the major rivers in Britain in second half of the nineteenth century where many of the fishing rights had been let to private individuals. The Salmon Fisheries inquiry of 1860-61 and the Game Laws Report of 1872-73 describe brutal clashes between poachers, bailiffs and watchers. The organised poaching of salmon along the upper and middle parts of the river Wye from the mid nineteenth century to the 1930s caused widespread concern among the authorities. David Jones characterises the conflict on the river Wye as the Second Rebecca Riots as it involved large gangs of men with blackened faces, bludgeons and guns.

Nationally, confrontations between poachers and water bailiffs and the police sometimes resulted in severe injuries and even deaths.[43] The conflict extended to areas of the river Wye bordering on the Forest of Dean between Lydbrook and Symonds Yat.[44] In addition, various other commissions and Inspector reports testified to the organised nature of poaching along the river Severn over this period.[45] Lord Fitzharding's Fishery on the River Severn near Blakeney was a particular target. In addition, in the same area, the Severn Board of Conservators had problems preventing the poaching of salmon out of season. Further up the river, around Gloucester, the authorities were facing a similar problem over the fishing of elvers (young eels).[46]

43 *Staffordshire Advertiser* 29 July 1854.

44 *South Wales Daily News* 03 August 1892 and *Gloucester Journal* 17 December 1881.

45 Jones,. D., The Second Rebecca riots, *Llafur,* Vol. 2, no. 1 (Spring 1976), p. 32-56.

46 In 1874 a law was passed prohibiting fishing for the 'elver' on the lower Severn. This resulted in conflict between the urban poor of Gloucester who had by custom claimed the right to fish for the elver and the Worcester Board of Conservators further up the river whose concern was the conservation of the eel. This conflict between customary rights and conservation in relation to elvers in the river severn fishery district is explored in Hunt, W. *The Victorian Elver Wars,* Cheltenham: Beardon. 2007.

Aftermath of the 1831 Riot

Despite the removal of the deer, the poaching of game continued in the Statutory Forest. However, the Crown's main concern was now the commoners and their sheep. After the 1831 riots, the question of the legal right to common was still disputed by both sides and this led to a war of attrition between the commoners and the Crown throughout the rest of the nineteenth century.

The 1831 riots did result in a number of concessions from the authorities for some sections of the Forest population. Some encroachers were granted leasehold or freehold of their properties. The Dean Forest (Mines) Act of 1838 confirmed the free miners' exclusive rights to the Forest's minerals, but permitted a galee (holder of a right to open and work a mine) to sell his gale (the right) to persons other than free miners.[47] It was this which allowed outside capitalists to move into the Forest and open deep pits.

Chris Fisher argues that the significance of this reform was that property rights were introduced to both mines and homes which displaced the egalitarian community of free miners with their strongly held beliefs in customary rights.[48] The ownership and the use of resources in the Forest had been fundamentally transformed in ways which favoured private property, the exchange of commodities for profit and the accumulation of capital for a few at the expense of the labouring many. No concessions were granted for the right to common where notions of customary right and community ran into direct conflict with the new notions of private property and individualism. The Crown continued to deny that there was a legal right to common whilst the commoners insisted they had this right through custom and privilege. Many Foresters were destitute and remained bitter after the transportation or imprisonment of the leaders of the uprising, particularly as many were sentenced by the courts to rebuild the enclosures as a punishment for tearing down the fences.

In June 1837, a meeting was called at Speech House in response to the Crown Commissioners' plans to extinguish the right to common. Hundreds of people turned up and gave a commitment to defend their heritage. A petition was organised which opposed the government's proposal. *The Gloucester Journal* reported:

> Three hundred signatures were affixed to the declaration before we left, but many thousands are expected to join the petition.[49]

47 A gale is a grant of specific seams of coal or deposits of iron ore or stone in a specific situation.
48 Fisher C. (2016) chapter 2.
49 *The Gloucester Journal* 1 July 1837.

In response to the petition, the Commissioners agreed to discontinue the regular temporary clearing of the animals from the Forest (drifts) at the Fence Month and the Winter Heyning.[50] One of the reasons for the drifts was to ascertain the number of animals in the Forest and to make the case that the commoners had no legal rights and were only allowed to run their animals on Crown land on sufferance. The keepers were told to drive only occasionally in order to keep up the Crown's right.[51] However the effect of this policy was to both encourage commoning and cause a persistent ill feeling between the Crown officials and Foresters. It was the drifts and the removal of animals from enclosed areas of Forest land which were fundamental to the conflict. This often involved impounding stock and levying fines on the commoners. Commoners continued to break down fences and open gates but animals were regularly rounded up and impounded. On some occasions animals died while being kept in the pound. In other instances violence broke out between the woodmen and the owners of the animals when attempts were made to rescue them. The Crown encouraged divisions between the crown woodmen and the commoners by allowing the woodmen to keep the fines collected.

At the same time, in the second half of the nineteenth century, there was a rapid development of deep mining in the Forest financed by outside capital. The majority of the Dean free miners had now become wage workers in the deep pits. Their coal and iron industry was now in the hands of strangers and the uses local people had made of the Forest were potentially outlawed.

The Forest under Campbell (1854-1893)

At the start of his appointment in 1854, Deputy Surveyor to the Commissioner of Woods, Sir James Campbell, set out to challenge the legality of the claims of the commoners. Campbell described the commoners as "lawless and disreputable persons who make no scruple as to any desperate act to gain their ends".[52] He argued it was difficult to obtain a conviction because:

> there are very many of the persons implicated in these transactions who, I am sorry to say, are as ready to make a false oath to defend each other, when brought to a court of justice, as they are to break down fences.[53]

50 The historical reasoning behind the 'winter heyning' was to keep commoners' animals off crown land in the winter so they would not compete for food with the King's deer when food was in short supply. The 'fence month' was around midsummer and animals were kept off to avoid disturbing the fawning of deer

51 Drift and Driving is the temporary removal of domestic animals from the Forest.

52 Deputy Surveyor to Commissioner of Woods, 3 May 1856, cited in Fisher, C. (2016) p. 146.

53 Ibid.

He went on to complain that miners, who were often also commoners, made holes in the fences as they walked through the woods from their homes to their pits. Campbell also claimed that only freeholders living in the parishes surrounding the Statutory Forest had the right to pasture their animals on Crown land. This excluded the many commoners who owned property within the Statutory Forest and those who only rented their houses. These tended to be the poorer members of the community. Finally Campbell argued that sheep were never among the animals allowed by the Crown to graze in the Forest and so should no longer be permitted on Crown land.

Sheep, which were harder than cattle to exclude from the enclosures, had become the dominant animal commoned. A drift, ordered by Campbell at the start of the winter heyning of 1864, found 5,868 sheep, 233 horned cattle, 218 horses and colts, 246 donkeys, 86 pigs, and 1 goat.[54] The keeping of just a few animals was widespread and so a large number of Foresters were involved in commoning. The drift was repeated in 1865 and caused some unrest and forcible rescues of impounded animals. At the time, the vicar of English Bicknor warned:

> It should be borne in mind that though this suffering may not manifest itself *openly;* the discontent which is come to be bred by it, may vent itself in mischief done by evil disposed people to the Crown property by *firing the young plantations.*[55]

As a result, the Commissioners of Woods in London, worried at the possibility of a serious outbreak of violence, persuaded Campbell to follow a more cautious policy in the following years. In fact, by this time more than half the enclosures had been thrown open as the maturity of the trees meant that they were judged to be safe from the damage of browsing animals.

In 1875, the government proposed a Bill to give the Crown the power to buy off all commoners' rights. The plan was to try and encourage the commoners to give up their collective rights and heritage in exchange for small individual private plots of land. This met with strong opposition in the Forest of Dean and nationally from the Commons Preservation Society which made a case for preserving Forests, not only for residents and commoners, but also for public enjoyment. [56] As a result the government abandoned the Bill. Similar battles

54 Deputy Surveyor to Commissioner of Woods, 1864 cited in Fisher, C. (2016) p. 143.

55 Vicar of English Bicknor to Commissioner of Woods, 12 December 1865 cited in Fisher, C. (1981) p. 151.

56 Standing, I. "The Forest of Dean: differing perspectives on its ownership, purpose and use", *New Regard*, Forest of Dean Local History Society 27 (2013), p. 5.

were being fought in other Crown Forests. In August 1883, G. E. Briscoe Eyre warned that:

> recent attacks made by the Office of Woods upon common rights in the New Forest – notwithstanding the settlement of 1877 – render it advisable that public attention should be called to the position of the New Forest, to its common rights, and to the value of those rights in their bearing, not only upon the interests of the locality, but upon the national economy.[57]

Working Conditions

Walter Virgo was born in 1845, into the heart of this conflict. His family were well known in the area and had probably run animals in the Forest for centuries. In 1856 Walter's father had run into trouble with the authorities for opening gates and breaking down fences. Probably, like most young boys in the Forest of Dean at this time, Walter would have worked in the pits and have faced appalling conditions there. The circumstances he faced as a child and as a young man are likely to have had a profound effect on his world view.

Among the biggest employers in the Forest at the time were the Crawshays who owned a number of pits and iron works. They lived in country estates surrounding the Blakeney area. They were incredibly powerful men and ran the Forest like it was their own fiefdom. Local men were regularly injured or killed in their pits and brought before the courts for poaching on their estates. It could be a mistake to cross them. This was the case for George Virgo, from Awre near Blakeney, who worked as a gardener for Henry Crawshay. After working for him for 12 years, Virgo stole a small number of potatoes and was brought before the courts. Consequently he was sentenced to one month of hard labour in prison.[58]

By the middle of the nineteenth century about half the population of the Forest was employed in coal works whilst the rest worked in the iron works, quarries or in the woods. Men employed in the deep pits were often paid by the truck system and many families were dependent on the meagre earnings they could get from running a few animals in the woods and the odd bit of poaching. [59]

In 1840 the government appointed a Commission to look into the employment of children in mines and factories. It found that poverty stricken

57 Briscoe-Eyre, G. E. *Briscoe-Eyre's New Forest*. London: Eyre and Spottiswoode, 1883, p. 5.

58 *Gloucester Journal* 12 December 1857.

59 Employers paid part or all of wages in the form of credit notes which could then only be exchanged in the employer's company or 'tommy' shops.

Group of miners or quarry workers in the Forest of Dean.

parents were often forced to send their children out to work and this was encouraged by the demand from employers for cheap child labour. Children as young as six were employed in Forest pits to pull trucks of coal along narrow underground passages which were too small for grown men. Many boys did not even get a rudimentary education because they could not attend school whilst there was work at the pit.[60] Women also worked in Forest mines dragging and carrying coal.[61] During the period 1850-1899 a total of 285 miners died in the Forest of Dean mines, including 50 children under the age of 16.[62]

As a result of the Commission, the employment underground of women and children under the age of ten was prohibited in law by 1842, but it was not until 1864 that these restrictions were extended to factories, foundries and blast furnaces. However, teenage boys continued to work in the pits and this often meant working seams 18 inches thick and dragging loads of coal through water along tunnels not much higher. In fact one of the Virgo boys from Blakeney Hill was seriously injured in a rock fall down a coal mine in 1870.[63] In November 1895 Walter Virgo's son Albert, who was seventeen years old, suffered a broken arm in an accident at New Fancy pit.[64]

60 Martyn, C. *The Forest of Dean Revisited*, Blakeney: Holborn House. 2015, p. 210.
61 Elijah Waring, Children's employment commission Report 1842, *On the Employment of Children and Young Persons in the Collieries and other Works in the Forest of Dean, and on the State, Condition, and the treatment of such Children and Young Persons.* (http://www.balmaiden.co.uk/FOD.htm).
62 Tuffey, D. *Roll of Honour, Mining and Quarry Fatalities in the Forest of Dean*, Forest of Dean Local History Society, 2006.
63 *Western Mail* 8 January 1870.
64 *Gloucester Citizen* 5 November 1895.

The Hod Boy is by John Wakefield and is situated between Soudley and Ruspidge. It was inspired by Erik Warren who was the last hod boy at Lightmoor Colliery who started work at the age of 13.

Unity between Commoners and Miners

Political tension had been increasing in the Forest for a number of years. In August 1842, three hundred colliers demonstrated at Mitcheldean for the distribution of relief after miners' delegates arrived from Staffordshire encouraging them to organise themselves into a trade union.[65] The same month, Ruffy Ridley, a Chartist orator, addressed large crowds at Cinderford Tump and Bilson, resulting in the meetings being broken up by the police and the arrest of Ridley.[66] The Tory candidate in the 1874 election, Mr Plunkett, was a relative and political ally of Deputy Surveyor Campbell. On polling day at Cinderford , antipathy to the Tory party led to people entering and leaving the Tory headquarters being pelted with herrings, the symbol of Tory resistance to the bettering of the working man's lot. This culminated in a riot during which the party's headquarters were ransacked and several houses were damaged.[67] The police had to call in reinforcements, officers patrolled the town with cutlasses and a battalion of infantry was held in reserve at Littledean. Over the next few

65 *Gloucester Journal* 20 August 1842.

66 Chief Constable to Home Office, 26 August 1842 cited in Fisher (2016) p. 59.

67 British History Online, *Forest of Dean Social life: A History of the County of Gloucester,* 1996, *Volume 5,* pp. 381-389.

days twenty-five alleged ringleaders were arrested by armed police officers led by Superintendent Chipp.[68] As a result, in early April, two men were sentenced to twelve months, two for eight months and one for three months hard labour.[69]

The underlying cause of the riot was the attempt by the coal owners to cut miners' wages and the Crown's threat to restrict grazing rights, both of which were supported by Plunkett. In an attempt to improve their conditions the miners had already begun to organise. In 1871, the Dean's first miners' trade union was formed and started to organise the men working for the outside capitalists in the deep pits. Edward Rymer was the full time agent for the Forest of Dean Miners Association (FDMA), from 1882 to 1886.[70] The FDMA sought to represent the men working in the larger pits. In 1883 Rymer argued that it was the duty of trade unions to defend the social, political and land rights of its members:

> When I wander through this beautiful old wood, and see the numerous pigs, sheep, goats, cows, horses, asses and poultry, grazing freely on the external produce found therein, I feel thankful that our men are at liberty to run their cattle free of costs or taxes, to help them meet the battle of life. I believe in the sacred principle, that God gave the earth to the human race for eternal inheritance, not to be taken away by man-made laws; and the man or men who would attempt to rob us of our God-given natural rights, must incur the danger of revolution, or other modes of popular resistance.[71]

Later on, in 1885, under the leadership of Sydney Elsom, the free miners adopted the model of the miners' trade union and formed branches all over the Forest. Elsom was a free miner, magistrate and methodist minister and was a much respected political figure in the Forest at the time. He called for unity between the free miners, those employed in the deep pits and the commoners. He also attacked the aristocracy, the Crown and its agents:

> There might have been some who labelled the miners, and men like them, as the residuum, the dregs, the scum but the most striking distinction between ourselves and our 'noble' calumniators is this–

68 *Gloucester Journal* 14 February 1874.
69 *Gloucester Journal* 11 April 1874.
70 The FDMA was the trade union representing the interests of the Forest of Dean miners and was affiliated to the Miners' Federation of Great Britain (MFGB). Each district of the MFGB had a full time miners' agent whose responsibility was the day to day running of the association, organisation and negotiations with the employers.
71 *Dean Forest Mercury* 14 September 1883.

> we have to toil day after day, year after year, work hard, live hard, and still remain poor, while they, as a rule, spend a life of idleness.[72]

The alliance of miners and commoners presented a broad united front to the Crown. In 1885 Elsom formed the Free miners', Freeholders' and Ratepayers' Protection Society. So from this date onwards the Crown had to deal with a committee which represented all those who stood to lose if the Crown had its way and whose attitudes and responses were informed by Elsom's sense of class injustice.[73] Elsom was very aware of Forest history. At a meeting of free miners in 1885, he reminded those present of past struggles in the seventeenth century and in 1831 and pointed out:

> that their old home had once been given right away bodily by the reigning monarch, and that it was fenced in and enclosed; but so great and determined an onslaught was made at the time by the inhabitants that all the fences were torn down and destroyed. He also maintained that fifty years ago Warren James had immortalised his fame by a similar feat of daring, which secured to the present generation their privileges.[74]

At the same time socialist ideas began to spread into the Forest from urban areas. National trade union leaders Ben Tillett and Thomas Mann spoke at a large rally in Gloucester in August 1893. They had been very influential in the huge wave of strikes and the rise of industrial militancy which arose in Bristol in 1889–1890 and the violent events surrounding 'Black Friday' in 1892.[75] Mann argued for a new unionism open to all workers including the skilled and unskilled, men and women and was influential in the growth of trade unionism in the deep pits. It found a home within the growing radical non-conformist congregation among the poorer sections of the Forest community including those working as day labourers in the pits. He argued "that the only reason they had poverty, crime, villainy, wretchedness, filthiness and the ignorance which followed from poverty was because of their lack of capacity to control the trade and commerce of the country."[76] He attacked the ruling classes and encouraged all workers to unite and take industrial action to improve their living and working conditions.

72 *Dean Forest Mercury* 13 June 1884.
73 *Dean Forest Mercury* 2 January 1885.
74 Ibid.
75 Backwell, D., Ball, R., Hunt, S. E., Richardson, M. *Strikers, Hobblers, Conchies and Reds, A Radical History of Bristol 1880-1939*, London: Breviary Stuff Publications, 2014.
76 *Gloucester Citizen* 8 August 1893.

Industrial Unrest

In the late nineteenth century employment in the Forest was very irregular and trade cycles produced booms and slumps. Disputes between miners and the owners of the deep pits continually erupted, resulting in strikes and lock outs in 1874-75, 1877, 1883, 1893 and 1895. The period lasting from 1873 to 1896 is often called the Long Depression.[77] The lockout of 1874-1875 was particularly harsh. In September 1874 the coal owners had attempted to impose a 10% cut in wages. The men came out on strike and remained out through the coldest winter in 25 years. Finally hardship and hunger forced them to compromise on a 5% reduction and they returned to work in February 1875 which was followed by another 5% cut in wages in July. The reduction in wages, the strike and consequent ill feeling between the coal owners and the miners was made worse by a slump which continued for the rest of the decade followed by the closure or sale of some pits in 1880.[78] Strikes often brought the miners into conflict with the local police.

> In 1877 miners at Lightmoor and Trafalgar Pits went on strike and police rushed to the collieries to head off a procession of striking colliers thought to be bent on mischief. In those days the magistracy included colliery owners and iron masters among their number and the strike weapon was not recognised as legitimate by many, including Superintendent Chipp. Though not used to break strikes, the police found themselves deployed to protect the mines from sabotage and strike breakers from assault and intimidation.[79]

Another strike erupted in March 1883 resulting in another lock out and defeat. In early 1893, the coal masters began to complain that other regions were undercutting their prices by reducing the wages of their workforces. So the Forest coal masters proposed cutting their own workers' wages by 20 % and restoring a formula called a 'sliding scale' which related the wage rates to the wholesale price of coal. The union refused to accept this, but in June the coal masters imposed a lock out and said they would not open the pits again unless the men accepted a 25% reduction in wages. This resulted in 4000 men being locked out. At a mass meeting at Speech House the men voted to stay out and refused to accept these terms.[80]

77 The longest economic contraction in modern history triggered by the Australian and US banking crisis in 1873

78 Anstis, R. *The Story of Parkend, A Forest of Dean Village*, Coleford: Lightmoor Press, 1982, chapter 8.

79 Sindrey, G. and Heath, T. (2000), p.19.

80 Anstis R. *Four Personalities from the Forest of Dean*, Coleford: Albion House,1996, pp. 263-264.

Meanwhile similar strikes and lockouts had spread to other coalfields in Britain involving over 400,000 men. Prime Minister Gladstone brought the mine owners and the national union together and a compromise settlement was achieved.[81] However by this time the miners in the Forest had been forced into submission and accepted the sliding scale, having returned to work at the end of October. Sporadic disputes continued. For example in the spring of 1894 the quarrymen were on strike while iron ore miners agreed to return to work with a 10% reduction in wages.[82] There was a bitter dispute at Speech House Hill Colliery in December 1895 when, following a reduction in wages, 517 men and boys were locked out. The dispute continued into the following year but in March 1896 the owners shut the mine down.

The majority of men involved in the Blakeney disturbances were colliers or quarrymen and would have been profoundly affected by these experiences. The census records show Walter Virgo's occupations as 1871 (collier), 1881 (collier), 1891 (collier) and 1901 (farmer). In 1875, he registered as a free miner at the Deputy Gavellers office.[83] However it is unclear whether he worked his own pit as a free miner or worked for an employer in one of the deep pits. Walter's sons were colliers as were many of the young men who became associated with the Blakeney disturbances. It is possible that many were working as casual day labourers for one of the buttymen who were self-employed contractors paid by the coal masters for the tonnage of coal they produced. The buttymen usually employed a small number of day men and boys as a casual labour force who would get the worst jobs for the least reward. Some of these men led a dual life as colliery day men and agricultural labourers. The union was controlled by the buttymen and as a result their employees may have felt alienated from the rhetoric of labourism and any form of political representation.

At the height of the Blakeney disturbances in the mid-1890s, the coal trade in the Forest had become even more depressed and many of the men could only get one or two days' work a week. In these circumstances subsistence activities such as commoning and poaching were probably essential for survival. Therefore it is no surprise that some sought to take matters into their own hands.

81 Williams, J. E. "The Miner's Lockout of 1893", *Society for the Study of Labour History Issue* 24 (1972).

82 *Gloucester Citizen* 19 May 1894.

83 The official register of free miners is kept by the Deputy Gaveller, the Crown officer responsible for the administration of free mining customs and the collection of mineral royalties. The Office of Gaveller is of ancient origin, and the Office of Gaveller in Dean Forest is of unique interest and has been handed down unbroken to the present day.

The Forest under Baylis (1893 -1906)

More serious trouble began with the appointment of a new Deputy Surveyor, Philip Baylis, who was determined to rid the Forest of commoners and their animals permanently. Tension was growing partly because "the number of sheep turned out in the Forest had increased enormously in the past few years".[84] By 1893, some new enclosures had been made, resulting in the total area enclosed amounting to 4,665 acres.[85] Baylis initially sought to extend the enclosures in the Forest up to the statutory 11,000 acre limit or more. It was precisely this issues that had caused the 1831 riots. If this happened the commoners would have to run their animals within the remaining woodland, forest waste and roadside verges which would put great pressure on the sheep owners to reduce their stock. Alternatively they would have to cut holes in the fences.

Commoning was carried out by large numbers of small flock holders, including individuals who had only a few animals. A census of sheep made in 1898 concluded that there were 10,851 sheep owned by 236 people, most owning fewer than 50.[86] This meant that there was a large number of families looking after relatively small numbers of sheep, all of whose livelihoods would be affected by a ban on commoning. In fact, the figures collected for the number of animals in the Forest are likely to underestimate the number of owners with just a few animals, as commoners could hide their animals at home in the days preceding the drift. The threat of a total ban on commoning meant that the strength of feeling against the proposed enclosures was growing and this was to boil over into outright rebellion in the Blakeney area.

Philip Baylis

84 Memorandum on the Depasturing of Sheep in Dean Forest, 8 December 1893 cited in Fisher (2016) p.161.

85 Memorandum on Drifts of Sheep in Dean Forest, 1893 cited in Fisher (2016) p.161

86 Deputy Surveyor to Commissioner of Woods, 7 June 1898 cited in Fisher (2016) p.144.

Walter Virgo

Walter Virgo's ancestors had lived around Blakeney for centuries and his large extended family would therefore have had strong roots within the local community. The 1891 census lists over two hundred people with the surname Virgo living in the Blakeney area. Walter's father James Virgo had occupations listed as 1841 (labourer), 1851 (farmer and agricultural labourer), 1861 (farmer and haulier), 1871 (agricultural labourer) and 1881 (farmer 11 acres). The family lived in a number of locations in the Blakeney area including Awre, Blakeney Hill, Viney Hill, Brains Green and East Dean and appeared to own small plots of land. James Virgo and Charlotte Yemm gave birth to Walter in 1845. Walter had six brothers and four sisters. He married Elisabeth Cooper in 1868 with whom he had eight children; John, Annie, Charles, Moses, Aaron, Albert, Mary and Walter. Elisabeth died in 1887 and then, in December 1889, Walter Virgo married Catherine Virgo, with whom he had one more child, Harold. Catherine Virgo was the widow of James Virgo who had died earlier on in 1889. James Virgo was not directly to Walter but lived nearby in old furnace bottom and worked as an agricultural labourer. Catherine's maiden name was Colclough.

The family attended an independent non-conformist chapel, the Blakeney Tabernacle.[87] There were a number of different radical and non-conformist religious sects based in the Yorkley and Blakeney area in the nineteenth century, some of whom rejected the hierarchy and authoritarianism implicit

1868. MARRIAGE solemnized at the Parish Church in the Parish of Awre in the County of Gloucester

No.	When Married.	Name and Surname.	Age.	Condition.	Rank or Profession.	Residence at the time of Marriage.	Father's Name and Surname.	Rank or Profession of Father.
199	November 9th	Walter Virgo	full age	Bachelor	Collier	Awre	James Virgo	Farmer
		Elizabeth Cooper	full age	Spinster		Awre	Wm Cooper	Labourer

Married in the Parish Church according to the Rites and Ceremonies of the Established Church after banns by me, E.R. Bolt[illegible] Curate

This Marriage was solemnized between us, Walter Virgo x his mark, Elizabeth Cooper x her mark; in the Presence of us, Jane Preston x her mark, Thomas Cadogan

Walter Virgo's marriage certificate.

87 Blakeney Tabernacle was originally sited at Brains Green and was held in trust by the trustees of the Hackney Theological Seminary, known as the "Village Itinerancy". The Tabernacle was opened "for the public worship of God" in 1823 when services were preached by the former curate of Trinity Church, Forest of Dean, who had "transgressed the bounds of discipline" and was no longer united "with any body of Christians". In December 1825 "a church was formed there of the Independent or Congregational Order" and was subsequently admitted to the Gloucestershire association of Independent Churches. In 1848 the Tabernacle was re-built and the new building was opened for worship again in 1849. (http://www.nationalarchives.gov.uk/A2A/records.aspx?cat=040-d5690&cid=-1&Gsm=2008-06-18#-1)

in conventional religion. Examples include the Primitive Methodists and some who based their beliefs on the religion of the Ranters which can be traced back to the English Civil War. These sects recruited within the poor communities of the Forest and were democratic and openly structured, often using lay preachers. Some attacked the prevailing social order which they felt was supported by the established churches.[88] It is hard to say what went on behind closed doors at the Blakeney Tabernacle during this period but people worshiping in their own chapel was a threat to a society which expected subordination and deference.

Walter Virgo's name starts to appear in court reports from about 1869. His offences include stealing wood from the forest, stealing sheep, carrying a gun without a licence, poaching, drunkenness and brawling Although all quite petty, they would have involved conflict with the local police. Throughout the 1890s, his sons John, Charles, Moses, Aaron and Albert and their associates appeared in court on a number of occasions for committing similar offences. During this period there was a sharp rise in petty crimes without a corresponding increase in arrests and this prompted the authorities to start to talk about the existence of an organised criminal gang.

Petty Crime

A consideration of some of the court records for the period 1880 -1900 for offences committed in the Blakeney area reveal a regular pattern of young men being hauled before the courts for poaching offences and other petty crimes. Most of these men were employed in the mines or quarries and some were repeat offenders who would become associated with the 'Blakeney Gang'. The appendix lists offences committed in the Blakeney area during this period involving these men.

Most were committing minor offences and hardly reveal the existence of an organised criminal network. An analysis of the table in the appendix reveals that the majority of these petty crimes reflect attempts to assert customary rights such as poaching, stealing wood and breaking down fences and so may be classified as social crime. When conflict occurred it was mainly with those in authority, who were attempting to challenge the assertion of these rights, such as the police, gamekeepers and bailiffs. A few offences were acts of pure criminality involving crimes against other members of the community such as theft of sheep from other commoners and assault.

88 For a discussion of the rise of non-conformism, primitive Methodism and the Ranters in nineteenth century Forest of Dean see Kear, A. *Bermuda Dick*, Lydney: Lightmoor Press. 2002 and Bright, T. *The Rise of Non-conformity in the Forest of Dean*, Forest of Dean Local History Society, 1953.

The majority of these petty crime offences were a result of poaching. Most poachers in the Forest were simply attempting to catch rabbits using ferrets and nets, although sometimes they were caught with guns in the pursuit of pheasants. As a result a considerable amount of time was spent at the Petty Sessions prosecuting cases of men seeking to supplement the poor diet of their families with rabbit meat. However, if caught and found guilty of night poaching, offenders could be sentenced to prison with hard labour or at least fined an amount that could leave the family short of food. Therefore it is no surprise that violence sometimes erupted when poachers were apprehended by the police, gamekeepers or woodmen.

Low level guerrilla warfare took place between gamekeepers and poachers on Russell Kerr's estate near Blakeney during the latter part of the nineteenth century. In March 1878, John Lewis, a labourer from Soudley, was caught in the company of two other men poaching for rabbits with nets on Kerr's land by his head gamekeeper Frederick Button and two other of Kerr's employees. When Button and his colleagues attempted to arrest the poachers they defended themselves with sticks and stones. Lewis was arrested while his colleagues managed to escape. Lewis was then brought before the magistrates and sent to prison for two months of hard labour.[89] However not all violent acts resulted in prosecution. For example, just before Christmas in 1883, a party of 'gentlemen' who had rented the shooting rights from the Crawshays at Abbotswood accidently shot and killed an 18 year old beater, Richard Williams, who was working for the shoot. No case was brought against 'the gentlemen'.[90]

Violent confrontations also took place on Lydney Park Estate owned by Charles Bathurst. In 1886, he let the whole of his extensive shooting preserves to Mr Dymock of Red Hill House, who employed a gamekeeper called Richard James to look after his interests. On the evening of 7 November 1886, a serious poaching affray occurred on the estate which left James badly injured. While feeding pheasants, James had heard a shot near one of the woods and set off in that direction. He then came across two men whom he suspected were well known poachers and asked to search them. The first man showed no opposition but the older man refused to be searched. James persisted and alleged the man knocked him down to the ground and that both men then proceeded to beat and kick him. James later claimed he heard the man say "Let us murder him" and then "I will put an end to you". Seriously injured, James made his way home and was given a lift to the doctor's surgery at Blakeney. He was found to

89 *Gloucester Citizen* 27 March 1878.

90 *Western Mail* 24 December 1883 and *Gloucester Journal* 29 December 1883.

Forest of Dean Colliers 1901.

be suffering from severe cuts about the face, head and neck, while his body was bruised all over. Some of his front teeth were knocked out.[91]

In his confused state James initially identified the men as known poachers Richard Beard and Philip James from Oldcroft. However, several days later the police arrested two men, George James (58) and John James (38), uncle and nephew of Viney Hill, near Blakeney when they were in the process of making preparations to abscond to South Wales. *The Gloucester Citizen* reported:

> They are known to the police in Dean Forest, and especially in the Yorkley District, as confirmed poachers and desperate characters. The record of offences against them is of an extensive and varied character. The elder prisoner a year or two ago made a murderous attack with a reaping hook upon two police officers who endeavoured to apprehend him on a charge of poaching. Both have served terms of imprisonment; and they are objects of terror to the whole of the surrounding district.[92]

The men were locked up at Lydney police station and then brought before the local magistrates where they were jointly charged with night poaching with a gun. They were further charged with unlawfully and maliciously wounding and causing grievous bodily harm to Jones and further with resisting and

91 *Bristol Mercury* 19 November 1886.
92 *The Gloucester Citizen* 11 November 1886.

preventing their lawful apprehension on the same date. They were sent to prison to await trial. In January, they appeared before Gloucestershire Quarter Sessions and were found guilty. George James was sentenced to twelve months hard labour and John James to six months hard labour.[93]

It is hard to estimate the degree of sympathy for such violent conduct in the Forest public houses where miners and other workers drank. A common representation of the nineteenth century poacher was as a romantic hero idolised by the rural poor with their exploits celebrated in the numerous ballads sung in public houses across rural England.[94] However the authorities were now warning the public of the threat posed by the emergence of so called criminal 'gangs' operating out of industrialised areas and the dangers of the poaching wars becoming more brutal and bloody.[95]

In reality, most poachers accepted their fate when apprehended. More often than not they were victims of a judicial system run by landowners who held deep prejudices against the rural poor and industrial workers. As a result, opposition to the draconian nature of the poaching laws was building within some sections of the Forest community. In February 1887, Sydney Elsom, who had been instrumental in setting up the Free miners', Freeholders' and Ratepayers' Protection Society, wrote a letter to the *London Daily News* complaining about the treatment of poachers. In response, the paper wrote a leading column supporting Elsom's argument. The letter was as follows:

> At the Coleford Police Court, Forest of Dean on Tuesday last, an old man named William Jones was summoned for having set traps to catch wood pigeons in the Crown enclosure near Sir James Campbell's. For this awful crime the poor old fellow was fined £2 and 11s. 6d. costs for poaching and under a second charge was fined £1 and 11s. 6d. costs for trespassing, or £4. 3s. in all. Jones did not pay these heavy, monstrously heavy fines, so was marched off to Gloucester Goal for two months. These heavy fines and this excessive term of imprisonment have stirred up considerable feeling in the locality, and Tory and Liberal are agreed that the punishment bears no proportion to the offence. So far as I know, Jones has never been before the magistrates before, and though he is somewhat eccentric in his ways, he is, I believe, a respectable old man.[96]

93 *The Western Mail* 7 January 1887.

94 Hopkins, H. (1985) p. 11.

95 Archer, J, E. "Poaching Gangs and Violence", *The British Journal of Criminology*, Vol. 39, No. 1. (1999).

96 *London Daily News* 9 February 1887. Archer, J, E. (1999) "Poaching Gangs and Violence", *The British Journal of Criminology*, Vol. 39, No. 1.

Members of the Virgo family were also caught up in this conflict. On 16 November 1892, Charles Virgo was caught poaching by a keeper in a Crown enclosure with Charles Edwards and William Reed, colliers from Blakeney. Virgo was caught with a gun, but made no attempt to resist, claiming they had never been there before. They were found guilty of trespassing in the pursuit of game. Virgo and Edwards were fined 10s and Reed 5s plus costs.[97]

Many Foresters had a dual life over the course of the year working as both colliery daymen and agricultural labourers. Farm workers wages fell by one third between 1875 and 1895.[98] Joseph Arch, leader of the new agricultural workers union, argued that "a pheasant is a more pampered creature than a peasant".[99] However hunger and poverty did not allow mitigation when faced with the interests of the landed gentry and their exclusive right to shoot game. As a result, increasing numbers of poverty stricken farm workers ended up in prison doing hard labour. In 1896, George Austin (nicknamed Dolly) and William Hampton (nicknamed Watty), both agricultural labourers from Aylburton were sent to prison for four months of hard labour for night poaching in Charles Bathurst's Lydney Park Estate.[100]

This was a time of a severe depression in the coal trade resulting in miners having their hours cut or being laid off completely. As a result many miners were now dependent on the proceeds of running their animals in the woods, farming their small plots of land or poaching to feed their families. At the same time the coal owners attempted to cut miners' wages further. This was the cause of the 1893 Lock Out which forced many mining families into extreme poverty.

Riot in Lydney

During the events leading up to the 1893 Miners' Lock Out emotions were running high, resulting in disorder on the evening of the Lydney fair in June. The disturbance was triggered when a local policeman, PC Albert Smith, intervened in a fight between Andrew Blunt from Yorkley and George Austin from Aylburton. As a result, Smith was assaulted by Blunt and some of his friends leading to the arrest of Blunt, William Cooper, Edwin Turner and Rueben James, all miners from Yorkley and Whitecroft. A riot then took place outside Lydney police station as a crowd attempted to release the prisoners. The magistrates at Lydney Petty Sessions sentenced Blunt to three months and the others to two months hard labour. During the trial the court heard a statement from Superintendant Ford and PC Clark that:

97 *Gloucester Journal* 26 November 1892.
98 Hopkins, H (1985) p. 282.
99 Hopkins, H (1985) p. 246.
100 *South Wales Daily News*, 24 September 1896.

> bore testimony to the extraordinary conduct on behalf of the public, and it appeared that about 2,000 persons were assembled, who made a demonstration in front of the police station, and threw stones, one of which hit the sergeant in the stomach. Such riotous conduct had never before been experienced in Lydney.[101]

The actions of the rioters were strongly condemned in a statement by Sir James Campbell. The following year, in December 1894, Aaron Jones and John James, colliers from Yorkley were summoned by William Howe, gamekeeper, for night poaching in Horage Wood, the property of Sir Charles Bathurst who had let the shooting rights to Chetwood Aiken of Bristol.[102] The court imposed draconian sentences which only succeeded in increasing the tension between the authorities and members of the mining community. Jones was fined 50s and £1 11s 6d costs, equivalent to about three month's wages. James was sent to prison for three months. On top of this both parties were required to be bound over for £10 each for good behaviour for a year.[103]

The Davis Family

Another family from the area causing problems for the authorities was headed by Henry Davis (Taffy) with his sons Edmund, Evan and Harvey. They all worked as fishermen living at Purlieu near Blakeney. Evan Davis was a close associate of Moses Virgo. In September 1889, Evan Davis was charged with maliciously damaging a gate on the property of Elisha Haile of Purton Farm and being abusive towards Haile. Davis claimed that it was his customary right to use the footpath as a route to the river Severn where he worked as a fisherman. He argued that it had been used for many years by the people of Blakeney, in particular fishermen, and called witnesses to support his claim. The magistrates argued that Davis would need to hire a solicitor to support his case and imposed a fine of 2s 6d and 1s damages and costs. The people of Blakeney followed the case with great interest as many of them used the footpath. However there is no evidence of Davis raising the funds to hire a solicitor and establishing his claim in law.[104]

In December 1891, Henry and Harvey Davis accompanied by Daniel Davies, a miner from Soudley, sailed their boat across the Severn to Arlingham and stole a dozen turkeys valued at £8 from J. Carter, a local farmer.[105] They

101 *Gloucester Citizen* 29 June 1893.

102 Chetwood Aiken lived in Westbury-on-Trym, Bristol and was a bank manager.

103 *Gloucester Citizen* 20 December 1894.

104 *Gloucester Journal* 28 September 1889.

105 *Gloucester Citizen* 19 December 1891.

A picture of Evan Davis, taken in 1901 when he was aged 28, with a Sturgeon he had caught in the Severn. Evan Davies married Martha Wickenden in 1895 and had four children.

were caught and Henry Davis and Daniel Davies were sentenced to two months in prison.

In June 1894, Henry Davis was charged with assaulting James Lee and his wife Clara. Lee was a gamekeeper on the Lydney Park Estate employed by Chetwood Aiken. At the same time Davis accused Lee of assaulting him but the magistrates dismissed this case. Davis was found guilty and sent to prison for two months for the assault on Mrs Lee. In addition, he was fined 5s costs for the assault on Mr Lee and bound over for £20 to keep the peace for 6 months or go to prison for another 14 days.[106] At the same Petty Sessions, Sidney Edmunds, a collier from Yorkley was fined 5s plus costs for trespassing on the land over which Aiken had the shooting rights.[107]

The activities of the Davis family indicate that the concept of social crime is sometimes problematic. Evan Davis had the support of the local community in his attempt to defend the right to access to the Severn for local fishermen. However this was probably not the case for the involvement of his family in night raids across the Severn and the use of violence. John Archer argues that nationally there was a link between those involved with poaching, a social

106 *Gloucester Citizen* 28 June 1894.
107 Ibid.

crime and those involved in criminal activity. In his study of poaching gangs and violence in Lancashire he suggests:

> the presence of individuals who included poaching as just one more act in their criminal repertoire of larceny and assault indicates that the concept of social crime requires qualification. It may be that poaching remains a social crime without the perpetrators always being social criminals. The Lancashire police clearly found that poaching gangs threatened more than just the existence of partridge, pheasant and hare. These gangs contributed to the growing belief in the dangers posed by the so-called criminal classes.[108]

Many of the men in the 'gang' socialised in pubs in the Blakeney and Yorkley area and the court records for minor drinking offences reveal that some of the men listed in the appendix were closely associated. It is clear from these reports that the Cock Inn, The Bird in Hand and The Travellers Rest in Blakeney were quite lively places where, it is likely, contacts were made, plans were hatched and produce bought and sold.

Accusations against Virgo

In December 1893, Walter Virgo was named as the defendant in a petition brought by Mrs Anne Adams for damages caused by his sheep in her vegetable garden. In a letter to the *Dean Forest Mercury* she said:

> I have not interfered with Forest rights or customs. But being only a humble cottager I have no right to speak for my own rights; I must keep silent, and have my garden overrun by a flock of sheep, 20 or 30 at a time, I suppose I must allow them to come and go as they choose, without interfering with them.[109]

A poor cottager could not generally afford legal fees and as a result Elsom suspected that the finances for this action were being provided by the new Deputy Surveyor, Baylis, in an attempt to provide a legal challenge to the right to common. In the end, Walter Virgo compensated Anne Adams for the damage his sheep did to her garden and so the case did not go to court.

At this time, Walter Virgo was in conflict with Baylis because the keepers had impounded some of his sheep which they claimed they had found within a Crown enclosure. The sheep were subsequently rescued in a night raid on the

108 Archer, J. E. (1999) p. 37.
109 *Dean Forest Mercury* 9 February 1894.

pound. Baylis ordered more of his sheep to be taken and a fine of 3 shillings on each of them with the result that Virgo uttered serious threats against one of the woodmen.[110] According to Baylis, Virgo and his relatives were altogether a "bad lot":

> This man Walter Virgo is one of a family that has a most notoriously bad character in the Forest–and I am informed that Walter Virgo has been convicted of sheep stealing and has also on two other occasions been tried at Gloster (*sic*) for offences but acquitted–and at present he and other members of his family exercise a system of terrorism over the inhabitants of the Forest and it is commonly stated that if other people incur their displeasure or turn animals out on the Forest by which the pasturage used by the Virgos would be lessened the animals are either driven over quarries–or killed or injured or some other injury inflicted.[111]

Baylis could not provide any concrete evidence to back up these accusations but sought to use the issue of the conflict in Blakeney to gain political advantage over the commoners. He falsely claimed that there were only a handful of large flock holders who were using the right to common. In particular, he focused his allegations against Walter Virgo.

Rebellion in Blakeney

Baylis's accusations against Virgo found support from Reverend A. D. Pringle of the Anglican All Saints Church, Viney Hill, whose parish adjoined Virgo territory in Blakeney Hill. Pringle wrote to the Commissioners in April 1895 to inform them of the maiming of two horses belonging to Mr. Butler, a draper, grocer and rate payer, which Pringle alleged had been committed by the Virgos. He reported that the 'gang' had grown in size in recent months. He claimed that their brutal deeds which included fowl stealing, robbing clothes, poisoning dogs, maiming sheep and destroying dogs and horses and had gone on for years and was now getting worse. It would surprise no-one, he wrote, if acts of violence "in defence of property" were to be committed.[112] In a letter to the *London Standard* he stated that "in exceptional lawlessness there ought to be exceptional law, for the conditions of affairs is worse than in Ireland."[113]

110 Deputy Surveyor to Commissioner of Woods, 19 May 1984 cited in Fisher (2016) p.158.
111 Ibid.
112 A. D. Pringle to Commissioner of Woods and Gloucester citizen, 30 April 1895 cited in Fisher (2016) p.159.
113 *London Standard* 8 May 1895 and *Gloucester Citizen* 9 May 1895.

He argued that the only way to stop these outrages was an outright ban on commoning.

There was no direct evidence linking this crime to the Virgos. However unenclosed land was not rateable and so rate payers had more to gain from Crown land being enclosed. This is because the newly enclosed land would then be subject to rates and so the average bill for individual ratepayers in the same area would then be reduced. As a result there was significant conflict between the commoners and rate payers over the right of common. Therefore it was reasonable to assume that this may have been the motive for the maiming of Butler's horses.

According to Baylis, the 'gang' had taken to going about at night in groups of twelve or thirteen, armed with bludgeons. He claimed that they were so numerous and well organised that they could keep a complete watch on the police, day and night and no sooner had the police stopped guarding a particular location the 'gang' moved in to commit some crime.[114] Meanwhile Walter Virgo was reported to have purchased two revolvers in Gloucester and Baylis warned that the "general opinion is that there will be serious murders as the outcome of the present state of things".[115] He argued that an overwhelming display of force, preferably a troop of cavalry patrolling day and night, was necessary. The situation was deemed so serious that the MP, Sir W. Wedderburn, asked in the House of Commons what the Home Office was doing about affairs in Blakeney.[116] The Chief Constable of Gloucestershire, Henry Christian, had already agreed to draft in an extra eight men for the night watch.[117]

The increased police surveillance resulted in clashes between police and local men. In April 1895, the sons of Walter Virgo, Aaron and Moses, and Evan Davis were walking towards the Swan Temperance Hotel in Blakeney near to midnight when they encountered some policemen, including PC Newport, who challenged them about the contents of the bag they were carrying. There followed a brawl between the members of the 'gang' and a number of police in which Newport and Aaron Virgo were injured. Convicted of assaulting Newport, the Virgo brothers received a one month prison sentence each and Davis a ten shilling fine.[118] It turned out that the bag contained stinging nettles. Baylis alleged that if there had not been other constables present Newport would have died in the assault.[119]

114 Deputy Surveyor to Commissioner of Woods, 15 May 1895 cited in Fisher (2016) p.159.

115 Ibid.

116 *Gloucester Citizen* 16 and 17 May 1895.

117 Chief Constable to Commissioner of Woods, 5 May 1895 cited in Fisher (2016) p.159.

118 *Gloucester Citizen* 4 May 1895.

119 Deputy Surveyor to Commissioner of Woods, 15 May 1895 cited in Fisher (2016) p.159.

Petition against the Gang

Both Elsom and Rowlinson, the new FDMA agent, were critical of the comments of Deputy Surveyor Baylis and his supporter Reverend Pringle. They accused them of becoming hysterical and vastly exaggerating the outrages to try and tar the whole Forest community with actions of a very small minority in an attempt to justify enclosing the Forest. They were aware that this was a concerted attempt to link criminality with the defence of customary rights. At the same time they both condemned the actions of the Blakeney men. Elsom had commented in 1894 that Baylis was "the most deadly foe Foresters have, as regard their local customs."[120] In May 1895, he argued that:

> to deliberately attempt to lead those who were strangers to the district to believe that the outrage at Blakeney, and the stealing of fowls in this locality, were the doings of a gang of ruffian Foresters, in the interests of pasturage or commonage, was monstrous.[121]

At a trade union meeting chaired by Elsom, Rowlinson observed "that it was not the first time the vicar had made wild statements about the Forest and Foresters".[122]

Also, in May 1895, the ratepayers of Blakeney Hill presented a petition to the authorities urging them to completely enclose the hill and to remove all the sheep. They argued that the Crown had the power to carry this out as there was only 6,000 acres under enclosure and they were legally entitled to further enclosures up to 11,000 acres. In fact the petition complaining about the 'gang' could only muster 26 signatories, all from wealthier rate payers. The petition also argued for the complete and permanent enclosure of all Crown land in the Forest.[123] Complete enclosure would seriously impact on the livelihood of the many Foresters who kept a small number of animals and so it is no surprise that the petition had little support among ordinary Foresters.

On 6 July 1895, a conference of Dean Forest Justices attended by Baylis and Elsom met with Stafford Howard, Commissioner of Woods and Forests, and expressed the view that enclosing Blakeney Hill and the surrounding Forest and the removal of sheep was the best way to prevent further misdeeds. The proposed area would include a thousand acres stretching from Blakeney to Cinderford. Other enclosures would follow at regular intervals up to the

120 *Dean Forest Mercury* 12 Jan 1894.

121 *Gloucester Citizen* 12 May1895.

122 Dean Forest *Mercury* 17 May 1895.

123 *Gloucester Citizen* 17 May 1895 and 28 May 1895.

maximum of 11,000 acres.[124] At a meeting of free miners in August 1895, Elsom commented that "it was very significant that about one thousand acres between Cinderford and Blakeney and the entire Forest near the latter place was the first district to be enclosed." However he went on to say that "the conduct of the men who had committed these outrages was devilish and fiendish in the extreme, and it was time it was ended". [125]

One month later, in September 1895, Henry, Harvey and Evan Davis were caught by PC Jones in the possession of an unseasonable salmon as they were landing their boat on the river Severn.[126] Jones informed them that he intended to take possession of the fish. Henry Davis replied that he had picked it up off the sands and he would die before he allowed Jones to take the fish. He then took a bottle from his pocket and threatened to hit Jones over the head with it. Jones then took the salmon and found wet lava nets in the boat.[127] Davis and his sons were then summoned by Charles Knight, the water bailiff of Newnham in the employ of the Severn Board of Conservators. They were fined £5 10s each plus 19s costs or one month in prison.[128]

During this period, there were a number of cases of local fishermen being brought before the courts for fishing for salmon during the closed season or using unlawful methods of fishing. Notices concerning fishing bye laws were posted in the *Gloucestershire Chronicle*. It is unlikely this paper was available in the Blakeney area. In addition many of these men could not read or write. The fishermen argued in court that new bye laws relating to fishing on the Severn had not been publicised effectively and so many of them were unaware of the exact details of changing regulations concerning the dates of the closed season and the type of nets allowed.[129]

Death of a Policeman

In November 1895, the involvement of the rural constabulary in the poaching wars resulted in a human tragedy. On the night of 9 November, a number of police and gamekeepers, working for local magistrate, Russell Kerr, decided to set a trap to try and catch some night poachers red handed on Kerr's land at Arams farm, Newnham. The team included Kerr's head gamekeeper, Frederick

124 *Gloucester Citizen* 6 July 1985.
125 *Gloucester Citizen* 12 August 1985.
126 The Salmon Fishery Act 1861 made it illegal to have in possession unseasonable salmon, or catching or attempting to catch salmon when spawning or near their spawning beds. Spawning is the production and laying of eggs.
127 Hand held lava nets were used to catch Salmon caught at low tides.
128 *Gloucester Citizen* 21 September 1895.
129 See *Gloucester Citizen* 14 October 1903 which details a similar case involving 13 fishermen from the Blakeney area including Evan and Harvey Davis.

Button, who had been involved in a number of violent incidents with local men. It was not unusual, at this time, for large landowners to treat the police as their own private security force in their conflicts with poachers. When the poachers came into the farm yard, the police and gamekeepers rushed them and caught colliers Joseph James (age 28) and Moses Virgo (age 24), with netting, pegs, sacks and four rabbits in their possession.[130] James James, alias 'Sheepskin', a quarryman, escaped. According to a report in the *Gloucester Citizen* on 15 November 1895:

> He can run like a hare and jumped like a steeplechaser. Whoever the man was, he led Keeper Button a fine dance. He cleared a hedge in good style, but the pursuer was "button" holed at this point, and the quarry got away. The police surrounded James' house at Old Furnace Bottom and, not finding him there, split into two parties, one of which was made up of Sergeant William Morris and PC Cornelius Harding.

Meanwhile three young colliers from Whitecroft and Pillowell had been for a night out in Blakeney after a football match and stopped at the Cock Inn at Nibley for a drink on the way home. They were James Morgan (age 24), his brother George Morgan (age 19) and George Hill (age 18). As they were walking home along Furnace Bottom, they were heard singing and shouting and ran into the two policemen at Viney Hill at about one o'clock. The police confronted the young men and told them to go home. This was followed by further confrontation and exchange of words leading to a violent struggle. According to PC Harding, George Morgan threw a stone hitting Sergeant Morris on the head resulting in a brain haemorrhage and death. PC Harding was knocked to the ground and the men ran off.[131] The men were arrested early the next morning and charged. Their injuries confirmed that they had been in a fight. They were charged with the wilful murder of Morris and the attempted murder of Harding. There was a great deal of public sympathy for the family of Sergeant Morris and a subscription fund was set up to raise money for them.[132]

130 For details of poaching techniques see Anonymous (1890) *The Confessions of a Poacher*, London, Leadenhall Press.

131 The events surrounding the death of Sergeant Morris were reported locally and regionally in the press. Details of the magisterial proceedings and inquest can be found in: *Gloucester Citizen* November 11,12, 13, 21, 22, 25, 26, 27, December 2 and *Western Daily Press* November 11, 12, 22, 26, 27.

132 Thomas, H. *The History of the Gloucestershire Constabulary,1839 -1985*, Gloucester: Alan Sutton, 1987.

On 16 November, Joseph James and Moses Virgo appeared in court charged with trespass and taking four rabbits. They were both found guilty. Virgo, who had three previous convictions, was sent to prison for three months. Joseph James, who had eight convictions against him for poaching, was sent to prison for one month.[133] On 20 November, the *Gloucester Citizen* reported that:

> James James, quarryman of Viney Woodside, Blakeney, better known as 'Sheepskin', a notorious character, who was wanted for poaching, was apprehended at his home this morning by PC Jones. The prisoner was found hiding between the joists in the ceiling upstairs, and was secured without trouble.

Sheepskin had only recently been released from prison after serving a one month sentence after he was discovered in a closed yard of a grocer's shop in Viney Hill.[134] On 22 November, he was sentenced to three months hard labour in prison.[135]

Sergeant William Morris (left).

On 27 November, the three young colliers accused of murder were removed to Gloucester goal by train. At Parkend a large crowd of colliers lined the station platform in support. The committal of the accused on a capital charge deepened the support of the mining community in their favour and soon a large fund was raised to cover their defence costs.[136] The trial took place at Gloucester Assizes on 18 February 1896. The evidence presented was often contradictory and Harding's evidence was open to question. On the night itself, the police were in plain clothes and it became clear that the defendants felt they were being attacked by strangers as they were not committing any crime at the time.

133 *Gloucester Citizen* 16 November 1895.
134 *Gloucester Journal* 25 May 1895.
135 *Gloucester Citizen* 22 November 1895.
136 *Gloucester Citizen* 27 November 1895.

George Morgan's injuries were quite serious and far worse than those of PC Harding, who admitted that he had struck the first blow. The defence argued that the defendants were justified in repelling "an unprovoked attack".

The jury found George Morgan guilty of manslaughter. A formal verdict of acquittal was returned in the case of the other two who pleaded guilty to common assault. George Morgan was sentenced to twelve months imprisonment, James Morgan to six months and Hill to one month.[137] Clearly this was a lenient sentence for the time partly because the judge viewed that there had been no concerted action on the part of these men. There is no evidence that the men involved in this tragedy were directly connected to the Blakeney disturbances. However the authorities used this incident to further their attacks on the commoners and the widespread reporting of the event linked it to the conflict in Blakeney.

Fowls, ducks and geese.

The arguments for and against complete enclosure of the Forest were debated across the Forest, in particular, at the committees managing local government institutions whose services were dependent on income from the rates. At a meeting of East Dean Council in January, Frederick Goold presented a proposal in favour of complete enclosure and argued that the extra money collected from the rates could be used to build more roads. Goold was a director of Foxes Bridge Colliery, a barrister and a member of a number of local government bodies. In response, the Council decided to postpone the matter until after the election of the new Council in April.[138]

A motion in favour of complete enclosure was put forward by Goold at a meeting of the Westbury Board of Guardians in February 1896. He argued that an increase in the revenue from rates resulting from complete enclosure would benefit the community as whole. The Reverend Pringle supported the motion and highlighted the events in Blakeney to argue that the right to common only benefited a small number of ruffian foresters. On the other hand, Martin Perkins, from the FDMA and President of Cinderford Co-operative Society, argued that complete enclosure would force the poorest members onto the rates for relief. He estimated that the extra money gained from the newly rateable enclosed land would not cover the extra cost of relief for those who would lose their means of support. The Reverend George pointed out that:

> these poor people could now turn their fowls and ducks and geese and they lived out of them. Then there were the cases of the poor

137 *Bristol Mercury* 19 February 1896.
138 *Gloucester Journal* 11 January 1896.

> colliers, injured at their work, who, if they could get hold of a pony or trap and turn the animal on the Forest, were also able to provide for themselves and their family. Again there was the case of the very small farmers who did not grow straw, who relied on the fern of the Forest for litter, and if the Forest were to be taken from these people what would become of them.[139]

The motion was passed with 17 votes in favour of enclosure to 9 against. The resolution was forwarded to Baylis, West Dean and East Dean Parish Councils, the County and Rural Councils, the local Liberal MP, Sir Charles Dilke and the Senior Commissioner of Woods and Forests, Stafford Howard. Dilke was elected MP for the Forest of Dean in 1892. He avoided making statements on this issue at this time, but he soon became a popular MP and an independent thinker, ready to defy the party whip on labour issues in support of the Forest miners.[140]

On 7 March 1896, a meeting of the Free miners', Freeholders' and Ratepayers' Protection Society was held at Speech House to make the case against Goold's proposal. The meeting was attended by over 300 people and highlighted the strength of feeling in the Forest against enclosure. Elsom presided over the meeting and in his introduction said:

> It has been stated that if half a dozen troublesome Foresters were removed very little would be heard again about maintaining the rights and privileges, which as a body they claimed, but the present meeting showed, what a delusion the people were under who held that opinion for even if some half-dozen were to be silenced, there would be scores of others willing to take their places, and ready to lead on the general body of men in the fight to retain their rights.[141]

Elsom concluded that it was the duty of all present to make sure they got the right men elected to the East Dean and West Dean Parish Councils in April, so that if Goold's proposal was presented it could be voted down. It was clear that the majority of working class Foresters, particularly in West Dean, were against the proposal and so no immediate attempt was made to put forward a motion in favour of enclosure at the Council meetings. Goold died in May 1897, but the debate rumbled through the Forest over the next couple of years as pressure was exerted on the Crown both by Elsom and his supporters in

139 *Gloucester Journal* 1 February 1896.

140 Dilke remained the MP for the Forest of Dean until his death in 1911.

141 *Gloucester Journal* 14 March 1896.

defence of the right to common and those for complete enclosure. [142] However, it was agreed that even if both East Dean and West Dean Councils decided that complete enclosure would be acceptable, a new Act of Parliament would still be required if the Crown was to enclose the Forest beyond the statutory limit of 11,000 acres.

Dynamite

The next significant event occurred when Baylis attempted to enclose part of Blakeney Hill and contracted Messrs Williams of Cinderford to carry out the fencing work. On 9 February 1898 at about 9 pm, residents in the area of Blackpool Bridge, including villages up to six miles away, heard three distinct explosions in rapid succession. The following morning, workmen employed by Williams discovered that the firm's steam sawing machine had been dynamited.[143] There was no evidence at all to suggest who had taken such extreme action but Baylis claimed he had no doubt the Virgos were to blame. Baylis was warned several times by the police about the danger to himself and agreed to leave the Forest for the time being. The Commissioners offered a reward of one hundred pounds for information but no one came forward and no arrests were made.[144]

As miners, the commoners from Blakeney had easy access to dynamite and this was not the first time dynamite had been used for political purposes in the Forest. During the 1877 miners' strike, dynamite was used to blow up the cottage of a strike breaker, Joseph Morris from Harry Hill.[145] During the 1883 strike, dynamite was used to blow up the houses of strike breakers including William Wilce from Ruardean Hill and John Smart from Brierley Green. Strike breakers returning to work for the Crawshays during the 1883 strike were greeted with a sign saying "Blood! Blood! Blood! If you got to work you had better make your wills".[146]

United Deep Colliery Gale

Although the free miners continued to work small drift mines which could access coal seams close to the surface, most did not have the capital to work the deep gales individually. As a result the Crown insisted on the gales being amalgamated in an attempt to attract outside capital to work them in partnership with the free miners. At the same time as the sawing machine

142 *Gloucester Journal* 22 May 1897.

143 *Bristol Mercury* 14 February 1898.

144 Chief Constable of Gloucestershire to Commissioner of Woods, 26 Feb 1898 cited in Fisher, C. (2016) p.160.

145 *Gloucestershire Chronicle* 17 February 1877.

146 *Gloucester Citizen* March 1883.

£100 REWARD.

Whereas on the night of the 9th of February, 1898, some person or persons did feloniously wreck, by DYNAMITE, near Blakeney Hill, in the Forest of Dean, a

STEAM SAWING MACHINE

This is to give Notice that the above Reward will be paid by the undersigned to any person who shall give such information as will lead to the Arrest and Conviction of the Offender or Offenders.

HENRY CHRISTIAN,
Chief Constable of Gloucestershire.

Chief Constable's Office,
Cheltenham, March 7th, 1898.

dynamite outrage, an important meeting of free miners was held at Speech House concerning the granting of the United Deep Colliery gale, estimated to contain 50 million tons of marketable coal, to a consortium of 901 free miners. However the depth of the seam and the finance required to access it was beyond the technical and financial capability of the free miners. The plan was to seek the financial support of outside business men who had the capital to sink shafts and pump out water.

The Cheltenham Chronicle reported on the well attended meeting convened by Elsom, who in his opening remarks referred to the dynamite incident near Blakeney:

> which he supposed was according to one of the local papers, to be the work of commoners. Upon what that superstition was based he could not for the life of him think, and indignantly repudiated the charge. He was sure there was not a man present who sympathised one bit with what had been done, but they all regarded it with indignation and abhorrence. [147]

The meeting then decided by a large majority in favour of the gale being held in trust by one individual. Later in the day Forster Brown, the Deputy Gaveller, met the applicants representing the 901 free miners and explained that the individual would be chosen by drawing lots. The result was that the gale would be granted to Walter Virgo to hold in trust. It is unclear what personal relationship Elsom had with the Virgos. However when making his comments about the dynamite incident it would have been likely he was aware that Walter Virgo was at the meeting. As a result of the draw the two men now had to work together in the interest of the community as a whole. In August 1898 Walter Virgo, as a free miner, applied to the Gaveller to have a gale granted to him to mine coal in a specified area near Parkend. It is unknown if Walter Virgo ever worked this gale but it was common at this time for free miners to acquire individual gales as an investment .[148]

Arson Attack

It was not long before another violent event outraged the authorities. On the morning of Sunday 3 April 1898, at about 1.30 am, one of the men on night duty at the New Fancy pit noticed a fire near the lodge in Russell's enclosure. He assumed that the lodge was burning and so went to help Hatton, the keeper, but found instead that the woods near the lodge were alight. Hatton and a

147 *The Cheltenham Chronicle* 19 February 1898.

148 *Gloucester Journal* 13 August 1898.

number of woodmen set to work to beat out the fire with branches. The *Dean Forest Guardian* reported that:

> It appears that the outbreak occurred at several places simultaneously, and no sooner had the men put out one blaze, than their attention was attracted to another, and this went on for hours, and in the opinion of one authority, somewhere before midnight on Saturday, somebody deliberately made at least thirty fires in the district referred to.[149]

Mr Baylis examined the burnt out areas and decided that no less than fifty separate fires had been started in the enclosures, most probably:

> by some person or persons carrying a small lamp such as miners use and just pushing it into the dry fern where there happened to be a suitable place.[150]

The fires extended over a line from two and a half to three miles long, on the windward side of the Forest, and must have been lighted by someone or persons who knew the paths of the Forest well. This was, the Commissioners wrote to their Solicitor, "a very determined attempt to burn the Forest."[151] Baylis said that if the wind had not died away and a light rain begun, the attempt would certainly have succeeded. Needless to say, Baylis thought this was the work of the 'Blakeney Gang'.

The dynamiting and the firing of the plantations had a clear political purpose. The saw machine belonged to the timber merchant who had the contract for fencing Blakeney Hill. In the week in which the explosions took place the machine had been moved to Cinderford Bridge to start the job. The fires were a direct action against the enclosing policy, a type of protest seen in the Forest before. If not social crimes, these were at least protest crimes with a political intent.

The Long Affray

Meanwhile the poaching war continued. In September 1898, Sidney Edmunds, David Beach and Frederick Jenkins, all colliers from Oldcroft near Blakeney, were charged with poaching in Purlieu Wood in Lydney Park Estate. Evidence was provided by William Wright and John Truman, gamekeepers for Charles Bathurst. The men were discovered kneeling in a rabbit warren, where a ferret

149 *Dean Forest Guardian* 8 April 1898.

150 Deputy Surveyor to Commissioner of Woods, 23 April 1898 cited in Fisher, C. (2016) p. 160.

151 Deputy Surveyor to Commissioner of Woods, 25 April 1898 cited in Fisher, C. (2016) p. 161.

was at work. The keepers claimed that Beach assaulted Truman with a stick. They reported that the men behaved so violently that they took to their heels and bolted. Superintendent Ford claimed that the defendants were of "bad character and gave the police a great deal of trouble". The defendants were found guilty and fined 5s each plus 2s 4d costs for poaching and 20s plus 24s costs for the assault.[152]

In October 1898, Sydney Edmunds and David Beach were in front of the magistrates again with their friend Frank Charles. This time they were charged with stealing tame rabbits and the assault of a police officer. At their hearing in front of Lydney magistrates Superintendent Ford opposed bail and said "Beach and Edmunds were old offenders and the prisoners and a few other men were a terror and pest to the neighbourhood".[153] At their subsequent trial at Gloucester Assizes, the judge commented that "they had received very severe treatment at the hands of the police" but went on to congratulate the police for doing their duty. Edmunds was sentenced to six months prison and Beach and Charles were sentenced to four months in prison. The reason given for the lesser sentence for Beach and Charles was that they had already been severely beaten by the police during their arrest, resulting in broken arms and head injuries. In contrast Edmunds had only received slight injuries.[154]

In November, William Norris nicknamed "Pit Hat" and John Charles, nicknamed "Jackice", both colliers from Oldcroft, were brought up from remand charged with night poaching in Lydney Park Estate where the shooting rights had been let to William Goddard Fitzwilliam of Ripple House, Awre. There was a further charge against Norris for assault as a result of throwing stones at PC Bick. The prisoners were convicted and fined £3 10s costs each for poaching and Norris was ordered to pay 28s 6d for the assault on PC Bick.[155] Pit Hat worked the morning shift at Princess Royal Colliery. In the early years of the twentieth century he gained a reputation for being one of the Forests' most notorious poachers. By 1931 he had collected five convictions for poaching including two for night poaching.[156]

152 *Gloucester Citizen* 1 September 1898.

153 *Bristol Mercury* 6 October 1898.

154 *Gloucester Citizen* 21 October 1898.

155 *Gloucester Citizen* 16 November 1899.

156 *Gloucester Citizen* 2 January 1931. He would eventually be sent to prison during World War Two when as an old man he only managed to turn up to one Home Guard Parade out of a possible thirty five. (*Gloucester Journal* 24 July 1941)

Moses Virgo

Sometimes rivalries arose between commoners. This was the case for Walter Virgo and John Virgo of Nibley Farm who were often in conflict over missing sheep, sometimes accusing each other of sheep stealing. Both were "considerable users of the right to turn out on the Forest".[157] As time went on Moses Virgo's reputation for drinking and brawling matched that of his father. On 15 July 1899, it was reported in the *Gloucester Citizen* that:

> Moses Virgo, of Blakeney Hill, labourer, was brought up in custody charged by P.S. Jones with being found drunk and disorderly on the premises of the Bird in Hand, Blakeney. He was further charged with being drunk while in charge of a horse at the same time and place. The defendant pleaded not guilty to each charge. The sergeant said that the defendant wanted to fight the best man in Blakeney. Eventually he left the premises and got on a pony, which he was too drunk to ride. He went on to say that he was trying to make an honest pound and that they were trying to make a rogue of him. The prisoner was fined 5s plus 16s costs.

In February 1899, another dynamite outrage occurred. In this case, the house of Henry Davis was blown up and the police suspected that it was a result of a dispute within the 'gang'. Davis received a number of broken ribs and other injuries while the other occupants of the house, including two women and a child, were uninjured. Moses Virgo was immediately arrested and charged. However he was subsequently released after producing an alibi proving he had spent the night at the White Hart in Mitcheldean. The police failed to find the culprit.[158]

The Commoners Get Organised

Baylis used the Blakeney outrages, the death of PC Morris and petty crime associated with poaching in the vicinity, to put pressure on the Commissioners to enclose the Forest. In particular, he attempted to divide the community by attacking the Virgos, arguing that they were the main beneficiaries of the right to common. When the Commissioners became aware of the large number of commoners with small flocks they realised they had been misled by Baylis. As a result, they responded by urging him to compromise. In June 1898, a memorandum by Stafford Howard, the Commissioner for Dean, marked the end of Baylis's ambition to have all the sheep removed from the Forest.

157 *Bristol Mercury* 6 June 1895.
158 *Cheltenham Chronicle* 18 February 1899.

> The number of persons keeping sheep as well as the number of the sheep themselves is very much larger than I had been led to expect, so that the matter will have to be dealt with very carefully and by degrees, no wholesale prohibition being in my opinion possible. It will be desirable to take means to let the owners of sheep know that their animals have no legal right in the forest but are only there on sufferance... Apart from this, and as long as the rightful commoners do not step in to prevent it, the Crown will not interfere with the sheep.[159]

In 1898, Baylis sought counsel's opinion before embarking on his new enclosures. A barrister concluded that the Act of 1668 confirmed the rights of the parishioners living in the parishes surrounding the Statutory Forest as claimed in 1634.[160] However they ruled out the acquisition of any right by prescription.[161] This means they ruled out the acquisition of any rights claimed as a result of the passage of time. Also, they ruled out the acquisition of any rights attached to encroachments within the statutory forest. He was less certain whether the claims of 1634 could be interpreted as excluding sheep. The Crown law officers, to whom the question was twice referred, agreed that there was no prima facie legal case for commoning sheep.[162] This was and still is disputed by the commoners who claim their rights are derived in law from custom.

Under the leadership of Elsom the commoners continued to campaign. During November and December 1898 fourteen meetings were held in the Forest where resolutions were passed in favour of maintaining their customary rights and Elsom suggested the formation of commoners' lodges to organise resistance to any new threats.[163] The commoners were now much more organised. However most now accepted that they could not overturn the Crown's right to gradually extend the enclosures up to the full 11,000 acres. At the same time, the Crown had been selling off small plots of land, reducing the total area of the Statutory Forest to about 19,000 acres. This reduced the land available for the commoners to run their sheep by about 3,000 acres.[164] In January 1899, the advantages of collecting rates from enclosure was raised again at the East Dean Council but the issue was not pursued.[165] Blakeney Hill North was enclosed in 1900.

159 Deputy Surveyor to Commissioner of Woods, 29 June 1898.
160 The Statutory Forest is extra-parochial.
161 Encroachment on Crown land, usually an illegal enclosure with a dwelling.
162 Hart, C. *The Commoners of the Dean Forest,* Lydney: Lightmoor Press, 2002, p. 146.
163 *Dean Forest Mercury* 18 December 1898.
164 Hart, C. (2002) p. 147.
165 Ibid.

The grave of Walter Virgo at the Blakeney Tabernacle.

At the turn of the century the sound of voices raised in disputes over enclosure in the Forest of Dean continued. For instance more conflict followed in 1905 when the impounding of animals found in the new enclosures near Whitecroft reawakened the issue.[166] A faction among the more wealthy ratepayers still wanted the complete extinction of commoning while Elsom insisted that the right should be preserved. However it was clear that by the beginning of the twentieth century sheep owners had not been successfully challenged and commoning had not been abolished.

Walter Virgo died in 1903 and is buried at the Blakeney Tabernacle. It is no surprise that the graves of a number of individuals associated with the Blakeney disturbances can be found in the grounds of this independent chapel as it was unlikely they would have attended the Anglican church of the Rev Pringle. Baylis died in 1906, a year in which the Crown Commissioners recorded that there were now 10,851 sheep running in the Forest, including 2,209 in the Blakeney area, which were there "by sufferance of the Crown and not by right".[167] Baylis was succeeded by V.E. Leese and by 1911 the enclosed woods had reached the full statutory 11,000 acres.

In the case of the United Deep Colliery Gale, Elsom worked hard to attract outside investors but had little success. In the end the free miners were forced to sell the gale for a pittance and forfeit their rights. This was another blow against those Foresters who sought to maintain their traditional and independent way of life and inevitably increased bitterness towards the Crown. [168]

166 British History Online, *Forest of Dean Social life: A History of the County of Gloucester,* Volume 5: Bledisloe Hundred, St. Briavels Hundred, The Forest of Dean, 1996 *pp. 354-377.*
167 Hart , C (2002) p. 154.
168 No immediate buyer was found but in 1901, Walter Virgo along with Sidney Elsom and another thirteen free miners were appointed to continue to represent the interests of 901 free miners as trustees of the United Deep Colliery gale. (*Gloucester Journal* 7 December 1901). In June 1907 the gale was sold to the Wallsend Colliery Ltd for £1620. This meant that the remaining 666 free miners were awarded £2. 8s each, 11 were awarded £2. 5s each and 59 were awarded 3s each. (*Gloucester Journal* 22 June 1907). Clearly these sums represented little by way of compensation and by now most of these men were working as wage labourers for the capitalists in the deep pits with an average weekly wage of about £1.

On the Severn the right to fish continued to be a source of conflict. In July 1908 the Berkeley police court heard a case involving Blakeney men fishing the Berkeley side of the Severn coming into conflict with bailiffs employed by Lord Fitzharding who claimed the area was part of his private fishery. Harvey Davis, George Virgo and others claimed that they had fished the channel for generations. However the judge found in favour of Fitzharding and the men were fined.[169]

Moses Virgo appeared in court on a number of occasions in the early years of the twentieth century, mainly for allowing his animals to stray on the public highway. He also spent time in prison for fighting and assault. Moses married Emily Virgo, who was not directly related, in 1901 and they had five children. He died in April 1938, perhaps by then reconciled with the idea that the old ways of doing things had gone forever.

Conclusion

Both Douglas Hay and John Archer have analysed the history of social crime and protest in Britain in the eighteenth and nineteenth centuries. Hay, in his research on eighteenth century poaching on Cannock Chase in Staffordshire, argues that the hatred of the rich and powerful often led to a:

> violence which was forced underground… that surfaced in isolated, anonymous acts of revenge which were among the few expressions of the labouring poor".[170]

Hobsbawn and Rude have highlighted how the penetration of capitalism deep into the countryside resulted in a wave of incendiarism during the massive agricultural disturbances known as the Swing riots earlier in the century.[171] The research of John Archer has shown that covert protest and social crime, such as arson and animal maiming, were constantly and persistently employed throughout rural England for much of the nineteenth century.[172] These sorts of actions clearly would be seen to be morally unacceptable today but in an

169 *Gloucester Journal* 4 July 1908.

170 Hay, D., et al (2012), p. 252.

171 Hobsbawn, E., and Rude, G. *Captain Swing*, London: Phoenix Press, 2001. During the Swing Riots of the early 1830s gangs of agricultural labourers throughout southern England burnt ricks and barns and destroyed threshing machines while threatening farmers, landlords and the clergy. They demanded a living wage, an abatement of tithes and an end to the hated threshing machines which had taken away their winter work.

172 Archer, J. E. *By a Flash and a Scare: Arson, animal maiming and poaching in East Anglia 1815-1870,* London: Breviary Stuff Publications, 1990.

historical context they provided a way for people with no political representation to exert pressure on landowners and authorities.

In the late nineteenth century, most Forest miners were excluded from all forms of political representation. Under the 1884 Representation of the People Act, only males occupying land or property with an annual rateable value of £10 could vote. Even the trade unions could not represent the interests of young miners as the FDMA was dominated by the buttymen who employed them as casual day labourers in the mines. There is a clear difference between overt collective disturbances such as the 1831 Dean riot and the sort of covert direct action which happened in Blakeney. An understanding of this has to take into account the unjust social relations and the isolation of the commoners after the riots which had generated such bitterness and recrimination. In the years following the 1831 riot, the fear of being caught would have led protesters to consider other tactics, particularly as the police were increasingly employed to enforce law and order.[173] So it is likely that the failure of collective action such as the 1831 Dean riots, and the repression which followed, contributed to the rise of covert action, particularly as all other avenues were closed down.

Resistance to enclosure in the 1890s took many forms, from petitioning, lobbying and civil disobedience through to violence, intimidation and arson. Simon Sandall argues that this long tradition of defending customary rights in the Forest of Dean would have existed in the collective memory of the community which had always used a variety of tactics. In most cases their actions were collective and social as opposed to individual acts of criminality. The most serious deeds did not lead to convictions and they involved a large number of local men who were well known. Therefore, it is likely they had the support of some sections of their community.

Some of the men associated with the Blakeney disturbances had a reputation for violence and it is possible that some form of intimidation was taking place against those sections of the community who opposed them. In addition, It was clear their actions did not have the full public support of community and trade union leaders such as Elsom and Rowlinson and certainly not the ratepayers in Blakeney who included shop keepers and tradesmen. So, if men involved in the disturbances had the support of other commoners, family members, friends and non-ratepayers from the Blakeney area then it is within this particular community that the concept of social crime had validity, but probably not in relation to the community as a whole.

173 The repression of the 'Swing Riots' was severe with nearly 2000 trials. As a result 252 people were sentenced to death (19 were actually executed), 644 imprisoned and nearly 500 transported to Australia for terms of 7 to 14 years with little hope of ever returning. This was the largest group of prisoners ever transported from England for a common crime. Ball, R. *Tolpuddle and Swing: The Flea and the Elephant,* Bristol Radical Pamphleteer #12, Bristol: BRHG, 2012.

We can conclude that the response and repertoire of actions of the Blakeney commoners was in keeping with their material conditions, access to political power, collective memory and belief in customary rights. We have to remember that Foresters had been operating clandestinely for years in order to survive and their actions were a result of enclosure and repression. This was not a state of their own choosing, the laws had been imposed from outside. Therefore, it is no surprise that they acted in a clandestine way and carried out the violent actions that they did.

An Organised Working Class

The militancy of some sections of the mining community in the Forest of Dean in the twentieth century had its roots in the radical tradition of the defence of customary rights which went back generations. Therefore it was likely that some of the strategies used by Foresters in the nineteenth century in defence of their customary rights would inform the tactics used in their later industrial struggles. Blackleg miners in the Forest were sometimes heckled and jeered by women and children banging old kettles, tins and other instruments. Forest miner, Alan Drew remembers such protests during the 1926 strike when "if they thought you were going back they would come outside your home and batter pans and tins and make a hell of a row."[174] This Skimmington style protest had its roots in a tradition which went back to the seventeenth century when it was often used against attempts to enclose the Forest.[175] In another case, during the 1926 strike, extra police had to be drafted in when a protest was mounted against blackleg miners working in a small pit near Whitecroft:

> They were met by an angry crowd of men, women and children, estimated to number 200, and were given a very hostile reception. Many of the demonstrators had possessed themselves of old kettles, tins and other "instruments," and as they accompanied the men in the direction of their homes these were vigorously rattled and banged, the din being almost indescribable.[176]

174 Anstis R. *Blood on Coal*, Lydney: Black Dwarf, 1999, p.112.

175 A Skimmington was a rowdy parade with effigies of victims, or people dressed up to represent them, to make a public demonstration of moral disapproval of the individual or individuals. The general intent was public humiliation of the victim(s). Skimmingtons were typically noisy affairs, with rough music made by the clattering of pots and pans

176 *Lydney Observer* quoted in Organ, D. M. *The Life and Times of David Richard Organ, Leading the Forest Miners' Struggle,* Cheltenham: Apex, 2011, p. 31.

In one incident in 1928 miners laid dynamite under the house of a manager at Princess Royal colliery after he had sacked a number of men.[177]

> Three blokes in Bream put a fuse they had, gelignite, under Burdess's house. They fused all under there (of course they were experienced miners who were blasting rock). They would have blown the house to Kingdom Come with him in it. After they had lit the fuse, they all went their separate ways, in the early hours of the morning. Trouble was his wife and children were in it. That was what one thought of, the one that went back. He thought 'Oh this yunt right,' and went back and put wet turf over it and put it out.[178]

Reuben James who had been imprisoned for his role in the Lydney riot of 1893 became an activist in the FDMA and in 1917 he was elected as President. As the twentieth century progressed, the working class in the Forest sought to improve their conditions and defend their rights through non-violent action and the development of a more democratic form of trade unionism, community organisation, peaceful protest and political representation. As a result the central role of trade unions, commoners' and free mining organizations, miners' clubs, brass bands and devotion to sport helped to create a distinct identity.

However, cases of poaching continued to appear in the local press throughout the twentieth century as some Foresters supplemented their diet with rabbit and fish. On 1 April 1921 miners across the country were locked out of the mines for three months when they refused to accept a huge reduction in wages. As a result some were forced by hunger to hunt for rabbits. On Tuesday 19 April 1921, forty miners from West Dean raided a rabbit warren using dogs and ferrets at Hagloe Park, near Blakeney belonging to Edward Mortimer Clissold.[179] As a result local miners Albert Edmunds, Albert Turley, Charles Norris, Edgar Norris, John Tay, Walter Turley and Reuben James were arrested by the local police. When spoken to, one of the defendants, a world war one veteran, said:

> If old Clissold isn't satisfied with this, he will have to lose more. We went out and fought for such as he. The rabbits are as much ours as his!

177 *Gloucester Journal* 30 January 1928.
178 Anstis R. (1999) p.108.
179 Clissold was a member of Gloucestershire County Council, Chair of Awre District Council and a JP.

Consequently, the defendants were brought before the magistrates and found guilty of day poaching. They were fined £2 each. A few weeks later Albert Edmunds and Reuben James were up in court for stealing chickens. Edmunds was sent to prison for three months of hard labour but James was found not guilty.[180]

Modern Times

In 1919, the commoners organised themselves in a protection society and a new Commoners' Association was formed. As a result, the Forestry Commission and commoners learned to live with each other and disputes were generally dealt with through negotiation.[181] Commoners remain an organised force today and the question of commoning in the Forest of Dean continues to be a controversial issue.

In 2001, the foot and mouth outbreak resulted in the cull of 5,500 commoner's sheep. Now there are less than 2000 sheep in the Forest. In February 2008, Commoner Jeremy Awdry was banned for five years from allowing his 500 sheep to enter a specific part of the village of Bream under the terms of an anti-social behaviour order (ASBO). In December 2008, Awdry spent the start of his 60th birthday in custody after being charged with 11 more breaches of his ASBO.[182] In October 2012, the minutes of a Verderer's meeting recorded some sheep had been found in the enclosures and, as a result, locked in the Forestry Commission pound:

> The Deputy Surveyor reported that 55 sheep had been lifted and two of the owners had paid for the release of their sheep from the pound, but the remaining sheep owned by Mr Awdry had disappeared from the pound and the alleged theft had been reported.[183]

Some politicians continue to exploit the existence of bad feeling, among a small section of the community, towards the commoners and their sheep which

180 *Gloucester Citizen* 29 June 1921.

181 Detailed studies are now taking place to identify areas which could be enclosed and grazed by cattle, horses and ponies which would ultimately improve the sites for the benefit of flowers and plants. Talks have already taken place with the Forestry Commission, Commoners Association and conservation bodies, including Natural England. The idea would be to open up some enclosures while fencing in others. The fenced areas would be for cattle and ultimately benefit from the grazing. Sheep and commoning will be encouraged to keep the bracken down on forest waste to allow the growth of wild flowers, etc.

182 December 2008 *Gloucester Citizen.*

183 A verderer is an elected Forest official with limited judicial power whose main duty is to guard the venison and vert. http://deanverderers.org.uk/

Members of the Commoners Association in the Forest of Dean in 2002.

recently has been aggravated by the irresponsible shepherding of one individual. In October 2015, the UKIP group on the Forest of Dean District Council, headed by Councillor Richard Leppington from Bream, threatened to bring forward a motion calling for the commoners to be billed for the cost of cleaning up after their sheep.[184] Consequently, in February 2016, the newly formed Forest of Dean District Council Irresponsible Shepherding Scrutiny Committee came up with some proposals to further restrict the right to common including a Public Space Protection Order (PSPO) to ban sheep from designated areas in Bream.[185] However, after a campaign, led by Mick Holder of the Commoners Association, the Council agreed in November 2016 that a PSPO would be too expensive and impractical to police.[186] Holder argued that the majority of the complaints were about the irresponsible shepherding of one individual from Bream who had been expelled from the Commoners' Association. He argued

184 *The Forest Review* 16 October 2015.
185 *BBC Gloucestershire* 25 February 2016.
186 *The Forest Review* 02 November 2016.

that Leppington and UKIP had been using the complaints resulting from the actions of this one individual to attack the right to common in the Forest of Dean as a whole.[187]

The deer were re-established in the Forest during World War Two and wild boar have been re-introduced into the woods in the last ten years, probably having escaped from a commercial farm. The deer and boar are regularly culled by the Forestry Commission in an attempt to keep numbers down. However poaching now provides an opportunity for lucrative rewards. In one case in November 2016, the grisly remains of a number of deer, shot by poachers, were discovered in a field near Staunton. Rumour has it that a good living can be made by using bait at night to tempt boar out of Crown land onto private land where the boar can be legally shot and then sold in London. However, the boar are sometimes shot and wounded or shot while in season when still caring for their young. As a result, the debate about poaching now centres on issues to do with conservation, animal cruelty and animal welfare. This is not to say that the odd pheasant from the estates which surround the Forest, doesn't end up as Sunday dinner for someone with an eye on a opportunity.

There are still a number of small drift mines worked by free miners today. But the threat to the remaining customary rights in the Forest of Dean still exists. In 2010 the Coalition government announced their intention to privatise the Forest of Dean which would have threatened free mining and the right to common. In response, in January 2011, three thousand Foresters marched in the snow through the forest to Speech House and burnt an effigy of Big Ben. The next day the image was on the front pages of the national newspapers. This triggered a national campaign, led by the Forest of Dean's Hands off Our Forest, and within a few months the government's proposals to privatise the whole public forest estate was defeated.

187 See letter in *The Forest Review* 16 November 2016.

Foresters March.

Appendix: Blakeney Gang Court Records 1870 -1899

Date	Name	Offence	Verdict	Penalty
11 September 1869	Walter Virgo	Assault	Guilty	One month in prison
25 July 1874	Henry Virgo, Walter Virgo, Samuel Virgo, Alfred Levis, William and John Wickenden	Riot and Assault of Bailiff	Not Guilty	
14 October 1874	Henry Virgo, Walter Virgo, Joseph Virgo, Samuel Virgo	Breaking down a fence belonging to Railway Co.	Guilty	Fined 5s each plus costs
27 May 1880	Walter Virgo	Theft of 2 sheep	Guilty	Six months prison with hard labour
1 November 1883	James James (Sheepskin), Charles Edmunds, George Edmunds and George Sanders	Poaching	Guilty	James fined 20s plus costs and the others 10s plus costs
10 January 1885	Walter Virgo, William Vaughan, Arthur Davis and John Newman	Allowing pigs to stray	Guilty	Fined 4s each plus 7s 5p costs
28 November 1885	Walter Virgo and Samuel Turley	Drunk and disorderly	Guilty	Fined 5s each plus costs
7 January 1887	George James and John James	Poaching and Assault	Guilty	George James 12 months and John James 6 months hard labour
12 February 1887	Walter Virgo	Stealing Wood from the Forest	Guilty	Fined 1s plus costs

Date	Name	Offence	Verdict	Penalty
13 April 1889	Walter Virgo	Stealing a ewe and fencing	Guilty	Bail and committed to the Assizes and fined 5s for fence
8 July 1889	Walter Virgo	Stealing a ewe	Not Guilty	
September 1889	Evan Davis	Damaging Gate	Guilty	Fined 2s 6d and 1s damages and costs.
11 January 1890	William Hewlett and William Windows	Poaching in Wensbury Wood	Guilty (Hewlett)	16 days in prison
22 November 1890	Walter Virgo, Charles Virgo and James Davies	Refusing to leave the Travellers Rest and being quarrelsome	Guilty	Each defendant fined 5 shillings plus costs or 5 days prison
8 August 1891	Henry Davis	Offence under the public house act for overcrowded house	Guilty	14 days notice to abate
1 January 1892	Henry Davis, Edmund Davis and Daniel Davies	Theft of Turkeys	Committed for trial at quarter sessions	Henry and Daniel Davis imprisoned for two months
25 June 1892	John and Aaron Virgo	Feloniously killing a donkey by driving into a quarry	Committed for trial at next quarter	Committed to quarter sessions and then acquitted
25 June 1892	James Virgo	Assault	Guilty	10s fine plus costs

Date	Name	Offence	Verdict	Penalty
6 August 1892	Henry Davis, Harvey Davis, Thomas Beddis, John Smallwood and George Golding	Affray. Drunk and disorderly	Not Guilty Guilty (Beddis, Smallwood and Golding)	Fined 5s plus costs each
18 March 1893	John Virgo	Theft of two wicker baskets	Guilty	Fined 10s plus costs
22 June 1893	Henry Harris (employee of Lord Fitzharding's Fishery)	Assault on Edmund Davis	Guilty	Fined 5 shillings and 12 shillings cost
26 October 1893	Walter Willetts and Henry Stephens	Poaching on Lydney Park Estate	Guilty	Fined 10 shillings plus 10 shillings cost
26 October 1893	Henry Davis, Edmund Davis and F Griffin	Poaching unseasonable salmon	Not Guilty	
26 October 1893	Edward Roberts	Poaching on Black Rock Farm	Guilty	Fined 5s plus 9s 6d costs
02 September 1895	Moses Virgo, Arthur Davies and William Vaughan	Allowed donkeys to stray		
2 May 1894	Evan Davis	Wilful perjury – accused gamekeeper of shooting his dog	Bound over to the sum of £50 and Referred to Assizes	
16 June 1894	Walter Virgo and John Virgo	Carrying a gun without a license	Guilty	Both fined 5s plus costs

Date	Name	Offence	Verdict	Penalty
28 June 1894	Henry Davis	Assault on gamekeeper and his wife at Lydney Park Estate	Guilty	Two months prison plus 5s fine
28 June 1894	Sidney Edmunds,	Trespass on Lydney Park Estate		
13 July 1894	William Bodenham	Poaching	Guilty	Fined 5 s plus costs
16 November 1894	James Davis and George Vaughan	Poaching	Guilty	Fined 1 pound each plus costs of 24s and 16s
08 December 1894	Sidney Edmunds. Warrants were issued for John James and John Powell on a similar charge	Poaching	Guilty	Fined 10s plus costs
20 December 1894	Aaron Jones and John James	Poaching	Guilty	Jones was fined 50s and £1 11s 6d costs. James was sent to prison for three months.
22 December 1894	Henry Davis	Theft of Holly	Case Dismissed	
4 May 1895	Moses Virgo, Aaron Virgo and Evan Davis	Assaulting a police officer	Guilty	Moses and Aaron sent to prison for one month and Davies fined 10s plus costs
21 September 1895	Henry Davis, Harvey Davis and Evan Davis	Poaching Unseasonable Salmon from River Severn	Guilty	Fined £5 pounds 10s each plus costs of 10s

Date	Name	Offence	Verdict	Penalty
16 November 1895	Moses Virgo and Joseph James	Poaching on property of R J Kerr	Guilty	Virgo 3 months prison James 1 month prison
22 November 1895	James James (Sheepskin)	Poaching on property of R J Kerr	Guilty	3 months prison and bound over for 6 months hard labour
18 April 1896	Moses and Albert Virgo	Theft of a chicken	Committed for trial at next quarter	Acquitted
02 May 1896	Walter Virgo	Unlicensed dog	Guilty	Fined 4s 6d plus costs
06 Feb 1896	Walter Virgo	Allowing cattle to stray On public highway	Guilty	Fined 2s 6d plus costs
18 April 1896	Walter Virgo	Drunk and Disorderly	Case dismissed	
2 January 1897	Harvey Davis, James Davis, Sidney Willets, Stephen Beard, Moses Virgo	Refusing to quit the Cock Inn	Guilty except James Davis	Bound over for £5 plus costs 10s
13 April 1897	Edward Virgo	Stealing a tame rabbit	guilty	Bound over for the sum of £10
05 June 1897	Walter Virgo and Moses Virgo	Allowing a horse to stray	Walter Guilty and Moses case adjourned	Walter fined 1s plus costs
30 September 1897	Moses Virgo	Using obscene language	Guilty	Fined 5s plus costs

Date	Name	Offence	Verdict	Penalty
13 April 1898	George Davies and Sarah Davies	Assaulting a police officer	Guilty	George Davies 3 months hard labour Sarah Davies remanded with friends or to be sent to workhouse
September 1898	Sidney Edmunds, David Beach and Fred Jenkins	Poaching	Guilty	Fined 5s each plus 2s 4d costs for poaching and 20s plus 24s costs for the assault.
24 September 1898	Edward Bent	Poaching	Guilty	Fined 20s plus costs
6 October 1898	Sidney Edmunds, David Beach and Frank Charles	Theft of tame rabbits and assaulting a police officer	Committed for trial at next quarter	Acquitted of theft Guilty of common assault. Edmunds 6 months prison. Beach and Charles 4 months in prison
November 1898	William Morris and John Charles	Poaching and Assault	Guilty	Fined £3 and 10s costs each for poaching and Morris was ordered to pay 28s 6d for the assault.
7 February 1899	Moses Virgo	Blowing up the house of Henry Davis with dynamite	Not Guilty	

Date	Name	Offence	Verdict	Penalty
15 July 1899	Moses Virgo	Drunk and disorderly while in charge of a horse and falling off horse	Guilty	Fined 5s plus 16s cots
30 September 1899	Walter Virgo	Fishing in Severn with unlicensed lava net	Guilty	Fined £3 plus 11s costs
23 November 1899	William Norris and John Charles	Poaching at Lydney Park and assaulting a police officer	Guilty	Fined £3 each plus costs of 10s and Norris fined 28s for assault
16 June 1900	Walter Virgo	Allowing horse to stray	Guilty	Fined 2s plus costs

Sources

Books and Journal Articles

Anonymous, *The Confessions of a Poacher,* London: Leadenhall Press,1890.

Anstis, R. *Warren James and Dean Forest Riots*, Coleford: Self-Published,1986.

Anstis, R. *The Story of Parkend, A Forest of Dean Village*, Coleford: Lightmoor Press, 1982.

Anstis R. *Four Personalities from the Forest of Dean*, Coleford: Albion House,1996.

Anstis R. *Blood on Coal*, Lydney: Black Dwarf, 1999.

Archer, J. E. *By a Flash and a Scare – Arson, animal maiming and poaching in East Anglia 1815-1870,* London: Breviary Stuff Publications, 1990.

Archer, J, E." Poaching Gangs and Violence", *The British Journal of Criminology*, Vol. 39, No. 1. (1999).

Backwell, D., Ball, R., Hunt, S. E., Richardson, M. *Strikers, Hobblers, Conchies and Reds, A Radical History of Bristol 1880-1939*, London: Breviary Stuff Publications, 2014.

Ball, R. *Tolpuddle and Swing: The Flea and the Elephant,* Bristol Radical Pamphleteer #12, Bristol: BRHG, 2012.

Birrell, J. "Aristocratic Poachers in the Forest of Dean: their methods, their quarry and their companions", *Transactions of the Bristol and Gloucestershire Archaeological Society*, Vol. 119 (2001).

Bright, T. *The Rise of Non-conformity in the Forest of Dean*, Forest of Dean Local History Society, 1953.

Briscoe-Eyre, G. E. *Briscoe-Eyre's New Forest*. London: Eyre and Spottiswoode, 1883.

British History Online, *Forest of Dean Social life: A History of the County of Gloucester*, 1996.

Bushaway, B. *By Rite: Custom, Ceremony and Community in England 1700-1880,* London: Breviary Stuff Publications, 2010.

Clark, S. *Social Origins of the Irish Land War*, Guildford: Princeton Legacy Library, 2014.

Elijah Waring, Children's employment commission Report 1842, *On the Employment of Children and Young Persons in the Collieries and other Works in the Forest of Dean, and on the State, Condition, and the treatment of such Children and Young Persons.*

Fisher, C. *The Independent Collier,* Sussex: Harvester Press, 1978.

Fisher C. *Custom, Work and Market Capitalism. The Forest of Dean Colliers, 1788-1888*. London: Breviary Stuff Publications, 2016.

Hart, C. *The Commoners of the Dean Forest,* Lydney: Lightmoor Press, 2002.

Hay, D., Linebaugh, P., Rule, J.G., Thompson, E.P. and C Winslow, C. *Albion's Fatal Tree: Crime and Society in Eighteenth-Century England,* London: Verso Press, 2012.

Hobsbawn, E. J. *Primitive Rebels: Studies in Archaic Forms of Social Movement in the 19th and 20th Centuries,* WW Norton, 1959.

Hobsbawn, E., and Rude, G. *Captain Swing,* London: Phoenix Press, 2001.

Hopkins, H. *The Long Affray, The Poaching Wars in Britain*, London: Faber and Faber, 1985.

Hunt, W. *The Victorian Elver Wars,* Cheltenham: Beardon. 2007.

Jones, D. Crime, Protest, Community and Police in Nineteenth Century Britain. London: Routledge. 1982.

Jones,. D., The Second Rebecca riots, *Llafur,* Vol. 2, no. 1 (Spring 1976), p. 32-56.

Kear, A. *Bermuda Dick*, Lydney: Lightmoor Press. 2002.

Linebaugh, P. *The London Hanged: Crime and Civil Society in the Eighteenth Century,* London: Verso Press. 2006.

Linebaugh, P. *The Magna Carta Manifesto*, London: University of California Press, 2008.

Martyn, C. *The Forest of Dean Revisited*, Blakeney: Holborn House. 2015.

Mills, S. *Poaching in the South West, The Berkeley Case*, Bristol: BRHG, 2015.

Organ, D. M. *The Life and Times of David Richard Organ, Leading the Forest Miners' Struggle,* Cheltenham: Apex, 2011.

Rackham, O. *The History of the Countryside*, London: Phoenix Press, 1986.

Sandall, S. *Custom and Popular Memory in the Forest of Dean 1550 – 1832,* Scholar Press, 2013.

Sharp, B. *In Contempt of All Authority – Rural Artisans and Riot in the West of*

England, 1586 -1660, London: Breviary Stuff Publications, 2010.

Sindrey, G. and Heath, T. *A Forest Beat, The Forest of Dean Police Force, 1839–2000*, Lydney: Black Dwarf Publications, 2000.

Standing, I. "The Forest of Dean: differing perspectives on its ownership, purpose and use", *New Regard*, Forest of Dean Local History Society 27 (2013).

Thomas, H. *The History of the Gloucestershire Constabulary,1839 -1985*, Gloucester: Alan Sutton, 1987.

Thompson, E. P. *Whigs and Hunters: The Origin of the Black Act,* London: Breviary Stuff Publications, 2013.

Thompson, E. P. *Customs in Common: Studies in Traditional Popular Culture,* New Press. 1993.

Tuffey, D. *Roll of Honour, Mining and Quarry Fatalities in the Forest of Dean,* Forest of Dean Local History Society, 2006.

Williams, J. E. "The Miner's Lockout of 1893", *Society for the Study of Labour History Issue* 24 (1972).

Wright I. *The Life and Times of Warren James – Free Miner of The Forest Of Dean* Bristol: BRHG, 2008.

Newspapers

Gloucester Journal
Gloucester Citizen
Gloucestershire Chronicle
Monmouthshire Beacon
Western Mail
Bristol Mercury
Dean Forest Mercury
London Daily News
South Wales Daily News
London Standard
Cheltenham Chronicle
Dean Forest Guardian
Gloucestershire Chronicle
The Forest Review

Picture Credits

Page ii - Walters, B. *The Forest of Dean,* Herts: The Temple Press, 1951, p.57.

Page 8 - E. G. Poacher's Companion, Woodbridge: Boydell, 1983, p227 (Bristol reference library)

Page 20 - www.sungreen.co.uk

Page 57 - The Commoners of Dean Forest by Cyril Hart, Lightmoor Press 2002

Page 34 - www.forest-of-dean.net

Acknowledgements

This pamphlet was a collective undertaking by a gang. Thanks to Chris Fisher for first discovering the story. Chris is now a sheep farmer in Australia. Thanks to members of the Virgo family from the Forest of Dean Family History society who sent me information. Also thanks to members of Bristol Radical History Group who offered invaluable advice and encouragement.